Charles E. Brewer
310 Falleson Rd.
Rochester, N.Y. 14612

SCIENCE
and the STATE in
GREECE AND ROME

SCIENCE
and the STATE in
GREECE AND ROME

Thomas W. Africa

John Wiley & Sons, Inc.
New York • *London* • *Sydney*

Library of Congress Catalog Card Number: 67-29015
Printed in the United States of America

Preface

This book is not a history of science but a study of scientists. It attempts to interpret the role of men of science in relation to the state in Greece and Rome. For comparative purposes, a cursory glimpse is taken at the managerial societies of the Near East and Far East. In the study of antiquity, conclusive evidence is not always available, and the sources are sometimes contradictory. Whenever practicable, the ancient sources are quoted. Footnotes are intended for utility rather than display, and extraneous digressions have been avoided. The book is intended not only for specialists but for readers who are interested in the problems of science and the state in any period.

I am grateful to the American Council of Learned Societies for providing a grant-in-aid for research on this subject. I also acknowledge the indispensable editorial assistance of my wife Ursula.

Thomas W. Africa

Contents

Contents

INTRODUCTION:

Scientists in Antiquity

When Euclid was asked what could be gained from the study of geometry, the great mathematician had his slave toss a coin to the inquirer. The legend reflects Hellenic contempt for commercialism and the annoyance of a "pure scientist" at men who seek an immediate profit in all endeavors. Today, the story has a fossil quality, because it depicts a form of life which no longer exists. In the modern world, science is a highly lucrative profession, as well as a means for understanding the universe. Sociologically, this development in science is of crucial significance, for the society of the future may well be a scientific temple state, if it is not a smoking ruin. The fate of mankind lies in the hands of physicists, chemists, biologists, and engineers, and the history of science in our parent culture, the Greco-Roman world, should be of some interest, because that society collapsed and science did not save it.

Throughout history, a few men have tried to understand the natural order of the physical world. Such individuals may be considered scientists, although many were engineers or technicians. Even our prehistoric ancestors were scientific to a degree, as they assembled specialized knowledge of flints and animal tracks. Later, farmers and artisans were protoscientists of a sort. Naturally, average men had little concern for the total order of nature or the abstract problems of investigation. With magic and religious rites, medicine men and priests tried to control the physical world, and they devised myths to explain natural phenomena, especially the awesome cycles of birth, growth, and death. With the development of organized urban societies, greater sophistication in science became possible, and significant advances were

1

made in mathematics, medicine, astronomy, and technology. However, science remained closely interlocked with religion, for the intelligentsia were usually priests and all men were religious. It is irrelevant that their explanations of nature were often wrong. In every era, scientists have tended to be conservative in temperament and attached to canons of opinion, for few men would embrace science as a vocation unless they were convinced that its methods and the current world view were true. Faith is essential for a scientist, whether he be a Babylonian priest or a twentieth century physicist. In the history of science, observation and experiment have usually followed in the wake of subjective preconceptions. Even chance has often played a significant role in scientific discoveries.[1] In antiquity, many scientists were priests, and by our standards most were superstitious, just as we may appear to our descendants.

To the historian, an astrologer is interchangeable with an astronomer if their contemporaries confused the two. Both the ancient astrologer and the modern astronomer have studied the order of the universe as prescribed by the conventional wisdom of their respective eras. The scientist entered history as a priest and departed in late antiquity as a functionary. In appearance, the roles did not differ much, but in relation to the state the difference was crucial. While the priest advised and counseled, the official served and obeyed, because his security and sustenance were derived from the state and not from the gods. Although Hellenic sages often dabbled in politics, the secular nature of classical Greek society excluded its scientists from the societal protections which were enjoyed by the managerial priesthoods of the ancient Near East. In the Hellenistic age, many scientists exchanged independence for the patronage of kings, and research was subsidized in Ptolemaic Egypt. The Romans had a high regard for medicine and mechanics but little interest in pure science. Nevertheless, the emperors continued the Hellenistic policy of sinecures and privileges for scientists, but Roman society eventually succumbed to a cloying religious revival. The intellectual climate of late antiquity became increasingly antirational, and science was submerged in a tide of occultism and religiosity. When the beleaguered Roman state placed itself under

Christian protection, priests returned to power but they were no longer scientists.

Since historical generalities are often misleading, a note of warning is in order. The eminent historian of science, Otto Neugebauer, states:

I do not consider it as the goal of historical writing to condense the complexity of historical processes into some kind of "digest" or "synthesis." On the contrary, I see the main purpose of historical studies in the unfolding of the stupendous wealth of phenomena which are connected with any phase of human history and thus to counteract the natural tendency toward oversimplification and philosophical constructions which are the faithful companions of ignorance.[2]

The point is well taken. However, interpretation and suggestion are the prerogatives of historians as it is the critic's duty to deflate hasty and ill-founded theorizing. Like the lawyer, the historian must deal with circumstantial evidence and contradictory witnesses. On occasion, historians may employ analogies with the qualification that "parallels are at best an invitation to thought."[3] In the philosophic sense, few historical statements are capable of absolute proof, but this is also true of most observations in the exact sciences. When the issue is as significant as the development of ancient science, even incomplete evidence warrants attention.

ONE

The Greek World

THE MANAGERIAL SOCIETIES

In a natural state, the life of man is "nasty, brutish, and short," but he is potentially a social animal. Grouped into families and tribes, primitive men could cope with a hostile environment, procure food, and fight off predatory neighbors. With greater organization, man produced civilization and created urban society with its complex demands upon the individual. The price that mankind paid for the better-than-animal life was the state. Wherever it is found in history, the state guarantees the economic surplus upon which civilization rests and off which the state feeds. In the most ancient civilized societies, a managerial elite—usually priests—directed the activities of the community. Whether the priests were the government (as in early Mesopotamia) or servants of the state (as in Egypt), the temper of society was managerial and the tone of administration was sacerdotal. Begun by the priests, writing and arithmetic were considered professional skills throughout antiquity. On the periphery of the Near East, the Greeks borrowed the scientific achievements of the older urban societies but did not adopt the managerial apparatus which had nurtured civilization in the dawn of history. A cursory comparison of scientists in the managerial societies may add perspective to a study of scientists in Greece and Rome.

In antiquity, the gods were never far from the affairs of men. Early kings were priests as well as magistrates, and the religious origins of Greek and Near Eastern drama are well known. In every nation, prayers were recited with great care, and altars

5

and temples were constructed according to specifications hallowed by custom. In the Vedic era, Indian geometry originated in ritual measurements for falcon-shaped altars which had to contain a specific number of bricks.[1] The Vedic priests were adept in peg-and-cord measurements and arrived at mathematical theories through trial and error. Throughout the ancient world, "the circle and square were sacred figures and were studied by the priests for the same reason they studied the stars, namely, to know their gods better."[2] According to the Seleucid envoy Megasthenes, Indian science was a monopoly of the powerful Brahman caste in the third century B.C.[3] Megasthenes also claimed that Indian scientists were exempt from forced labor and met annually in a great conclave to advise the state on impending droughts, public health, and other matters of import. As an adviser to the state, a sage was permitted three errors before he was banished to a "life of silence."[4] While Brahmanic birth was a prerequisite for scientific status,[5] the brain trust of ancient India retained its privileges by demonstrated competence. Men of ability were expected to place their learning at the service of society, and their careers were destroyed when their predictions failed to materialize.

A hemisphere away in Central America, the Mayans developed a full-blown managerial society which was dominated by priestly astronomers. In the Mayan city states, priests held power through their knowledge of calendars and were believed to be in contact with the vegetation deities who were cherished by the peasantry. However, the priestly elite was preoccupied with astrological studies and the enjoyment of power, and they often neglected the needs of the farmers. In the ninth century A.D., the Central Mayan peasants rose against the scientific ruling class. According to the archeologist J. E. Thompson:

[The revolt] may have been caused by the ever growing demands for service in construction work and in the production of food for an increasing number of nonproducers. Exotic religious developments, such as the cult of the planet Venus, adopted by the hierarchy may have driven a wedge between the two groups, making the peasants feel that the hierarchy was no longer performing its main function, that of propitiating the gods of the soil in whom alone they heartily believed.[6]

The alienation of stargazing scientists from the uncomprehending masses, whose labors support the privileges of the elite, is not a problem confined to Mayan society.

In the Far East, a great managerial society flourished in Han China, where astronomy and politics were hopelessly entangled, to the detriment of science. To the Chinese, extraordinary celestial and terrestrial phenomena indicated that the order of nature had been disturbed by misdeeds of the emperor and his court. The interpreters of portents often utilized their official position to criticize the regime and did not hesitate to forge reports of eclipses. In retaliation, the imperial government considered novel scientific ideas and practices as politically subversive.[7] In the opinion of the Sinologist Wolfram Eberhard:

Just as the astronomers, astrologists, or meteorologists were motivated by an interest not so much in science as in politics, so the government sponsored these scientific fields only in so far as they were politically loyal, i.e., as long as they did not develop new ideas. New ideas were conceived as new tools for the political struggle and therefore suspect.[8]

The political aspects of astronomy continued into the T'ang dynasty, when scholars and even candidates for the position of court astronomer were prohibited from contact with the dangerous instruments of science. In 840 A.D., the emperor Wu Tsung expressed his concern over subversive scientists:

If we hear of any intercourse between the astronomical officials or their subordinates and officials of other government departments or miscellaneous common people, it will be regarded as a violation of security regulations which should be strictly adhered to. From now onwards, therefore, the astronomical officials are on no account to mix with civil servants and common people in general. Let the Censorate look to it.[9]

The uneasy regime also persecuted alien creeds, Christianity and Manicheanism, but rigid security regulations did not prevent the T'ang dynasty from collapsing within a few decades after Wu Tsung's rescript on astronomy.

Under Chinese absolutism, the social sciences fared worse

than the exact sciences. In 213 B.C., the ruthless unifier of China, Ch'in Shih Huang Ti, had decreed

that all historical records, save those of Ch'in, be burned; . . . that all people who . . . discuss history be executed; that all those who raise their voice against the present government in the name of antiquity be beheaded together with their families; . . . that only books of medicine, divination, agriculture, and arboriculture be preserved.[10]

Like the Han astronomers, the proscribed historians had brought about their own plight, for they had manipulated the history of ancient China with a Confucian bias.* The Han dynasty execrated the memory of Ch'in Shih Huang Ti but also kept a firm control over the dangerous discipline of history. When the historian Ssu-ma Ch'ien deviated from the official court version of a recent military defeat, the emperor Han Wu Ti had the dissident writer castrated. "Each time I think of this shame," Ssu-ma Ch'ien confessed, "the sweat pours from my back and soaks my robe. I am now no more than a servant in a harem. . . . I follow along with the vulgar, floating and sinking, bobbing up and down with the times, sharing their delusion and madness." [11] The emasculation of China's greatest historian symbolized the plight of the literati then and now.

While the Greeks were unaware of the achievements and problems of scientists in China and Central America, Egypt and Mesopotamia were close at hand and awesomely old. Through most of history, men have venerated the remote past and sought authority in ancient sages—if need be, in forgeries which purported to come from antiquity. The intellectual reputation of the Near East was so overwhelming that Hellenic scholars gave undue credit to the archaic wisdom of the priests of Memphis and Babylon. With excessive patriotism, the Syrian Stoic Posidonius attributed the atomic theory to a Phoenician sage, Mochus of Sidon, who lived before the Trojan War.[12] In Egypt, Greek

* Many despots have tried to alter history by burning historical books. The Tenochcan ruler Itzcoatl destroyed the historical records of the Aztec past, and Orwell's 1984 manipulators of history have counterparts in many modern states.

tourists were treated as errant schoolboys by their priestly guides. Although many priests were pompous poseurs, one factor impressed discerning Greek observers: the privileges of Near Eastern intellectuals were remnants of former political and social power. The Greek historian Polybius remarked that "the Egyptian priests, the Chaldaean astrologers, and the Magi obtained positions of leadership and respect because they surpassed their fellows in knowledge."[13] In general, Polybius' inference was correct.

According to the historian Herodotus, geometry was developed in Egypt because the priests had to accurately measure farmland after the annual Nile floods.[14] In a similar vein, Karl Marx claimed that "the necessity for predicting the rise and fall of the Nile created Egyptian astronomy and with it the dominion of the priests as directors of agriculture."[15] Although the practical origins of astronomy are plausible, the priestly managers did not control Egypt as a sacerdotal oligarchy. In early Egypt the monarchy created and dominated the managerial class, which supervised the spiritual and material life of the masses. By the Third Dynasty, priestly astronomers had devised a 365 day calendar that was based on the heliacal rising of the star Sirius shortly before the annual inundation of the Nile. According to Plutarch, the priests believed that Sirius was "the bringer of water."[16] When the star was observed on the eastern horizon at dawn, the astronomers informed the king who, with great pomp, ordered the Nile to rise and water the fields of his awestruck subjects.[17] As a reward for these services, the priestly colleges were exempt from taxes and forced labor.[18]

The role of the priesthood in the power structure of ancient Egypt was typical of managerial specialists in a religious age. In his study of oriental despotism, Karl Wittfogel states:

The operations of time keeping and scientific measuring and counting were performed by official dignitaries or by priestly (or secular) specialists attached to the hydraulic regime. Wrapped in a cloak of magic and astrology and hedged with profound secrecy, these mathematical and astronomical operations became the means both for improving hydraulic production and bulwarking the superior power of the hydraulic leaders.[19]

Although his equation of hydraulic society with oriental despotism is too rigid, Wittfogel's evaluation of the priestly astronomers is substantially correct. In the pyramid of Egyptian bureaucracy, men of learning held a position of great privilege and potential power.

In Egypt, even the lowliest scribe was transformed by the aura of specialization. A famous text warned schoolboys to attend to their studies:

You should set your heart on books. I have seen the man who is set free from forced labour. Nothing surpasses books. . . . Would that I might make you love books more than your mother. . . . It is greater than any calling. . . . Never have I seen a sculptor or a goldsmith on an official errand. But I have seen the smith at his task at the mouth of his furnace. His fingers were like stuff from crocodiles; he stank more than the offal of fishes. . . . There is no calling that is without a director except that of the scribe.[20]

Protected and pampered, the literati of Egypt served the state and were rewarded by it. In the Old and Middle Kingdoms, Egyptians enjoyed considerable social mobility, for education was available for any intelligent boy who wished to escape from drudgery and devote his life to bureaucracy. In the service of the king, scientists and engineers identified themselves with the state rather than with the weary masses from whom they had often emerged. In ancient Egypt, the model civil servant was the "silent man," who avoided controversy and dutifully waited for his superiors to express their opinions first.

Before the rise of Greek medicine, Egyptian physicians were justly renowned.[21] Under King Zoser in the Third Dynasty, the vizier Imhotep was a magician, engineer, architect, and physician. In the latter role, Imhotep was so successful that at death he was deified as a god of medicine. When Ptolemy V ruled Egypt two and a half millennia later, the cult of Imhotep was still flourishing.[22] Egyptian medicine awed the early Greeks, and Homer acknowledged that "the Egyptians are skilled beyond all men in the healing arts." [23] Under Persian occupation, the status of the physician in Egypt was still enviable. The priestly politician Uzahor-resenet was commissioned by Darius the Great to restore the House of Life, the medical school at Sais. Uzahor-resenet later boasted:

I did what his majesty had commanded. I furnished all their staffs, sons of prominent men, not a poor man's son among them. . . . I placed them in the charge of every learned man. . . . I gave them every useful thing and all their instruments indicated by the writings, as they had been before.[24]

The social mobility that characterized the medical profession earlier in Egypt had been superseded by class concepts which were tantamount to caste restrictions. The exclusiveness of the medical school at Sais was symptomatic of the waning vigor of Egyptian medicine, which was unable to compete with its Greek counterpart. At the court of Darius, Egyptian doctors were soon replaced by the Greek physician Democedes, who was the pride of the medical school at Croton.

In the East lay Mesopotamia, the Eden of the managerial system. Unlike the Egyptian bureaucrats, the priests of Mesopotamia had preceded the secular state and had directed the work gangs who won the land from the raging rivers. Extensive irrigation increased the food supply, populations expanded, and simple villages evolved into urban centers. Armed with mathematics and writing, the priests created an imposing society of temple states, which depended economically on irrigation and trade. Increasing warfare between the cities of early Mesopotamia precipitated the rise of secular rulers, who curbed the political power of the priests but left them pampered and privileged.

Hedged in by magic and ignorance, Mesopotamian medicine was less advanced than that of Egypt.[25] However, Mesopotamia provided an interesting example of early medical legislation. At Babylon, King Hammurabi fixed the fees of physicians and punished their mistakes:

If a physician performs a major operation on a noble with a bronze lancet and has saved his life or opens the eye socket of a noble with a bronze lancet and saves his sight, he shall receive ten shekels of silver. If the patient is a commoner, the doctor shall receive five shekels. If the patient is the slave of a noble, the owner shall give two shekels of silver to the physician.
If a physician performs a major operation on a noble with a bronze lancet and causes the noble's death or opens the eye socket of a

noble and blinds his eye, the physician shall lose his hand. If a slave of a commoner dies because of an operation, the doctor shall make good slave for slave. If he destroys the eye of a slave during an operation, the physician shall pay one-half of the slave's value in silver. When a physician sets a noble's broken bone or has healed a sprained tendon, the patient shall give five shekels of silver to the physician. If the patient was a commoner, he shall give the doctor three shekels of silver. If the patient was the slave of a noble, the owner shall give two shekels of silver to the physician.[26]

The law code of Hammurabi reflected the rigid class lines of Babylonian society and insisted that a physician was answerable to the community.

Throughout antiquity, the Mesopotamians were renowned for their scientific skills,* especially in astrology. To Greek and Roman writers, the scientists of Mesopotamia were a hereditary caste, the Chaldaeans,[27] who scanned the skies for signs of national import and possible doom.[28] In early Mesopotamia, stargazers were not practitioners of horoscopic astrology, which deals with the presumed influences of planets and constellations on individuals at the moment of conception or birth. (Horoscopic astrology did not develop in the Near East until the fifth century B.C.[29]) Ancient Near Eastern astrologers were concerned with "judicial astrology," in which celestial phenomena were believed to reveal the fates of nations and their rulers. Since the practice continued for millennia, successful prophets must have had more mundane sources of information than the distant skies. Awed by the claims of Berossus and other Hellenistic experts on the Mesopotamian past, Roman scholars believed that the astronomical activity of the Chaldaeans reached back 730,000 years—Cicero's brother, Quintus, accepted a minimum of 470,000 years.[30] Understandably, Chaldaean science rated high in Roman eyes.

Actually, the most venerable "science" in the Near East was haruspication, the detailed study of livers of sacrificed animals. The Babylonians assumed that the microcosm of the liver reflected the macrocosm of the universe. They divided the liver

* In fact, Babylonian mathematicians did invent place value notation and discovered the so-called Pythagorean theorem in the second millennium B.C.

into sections, which were under the influence of gods who presided over corresponding regions of the earth or sky. Clay models of significant livers were kept for reference in libraries, and the practice of liver analysis was widespread in the Near East.[31] Through the Etruscans, who migrated from Asia Minor to Italy, the Romans were converted to liver divination. The haruspex or liver analyst played a major role in Roman religion and politics. The great antiquity of the practice and its longevity at Rome suggests that the haruspices relied more on common sense than on livers in predicting the future.

Fortified by piety and sanctified by age, Near Eastern scientists basked in the patronage of the state, which they protected from real and imaginary ills. Among the Assyrians, court scientists recorded eclipses and practiced divination. The managerial entourage of the Assyrian monarch Esarhaddon was listed in a report on loyalty oaths: "May Nabu and Marduk bless the king, my lord. The scribes, the seers, the magicians, the physicians, the bird gazers, the courtiers, residing in the city, took the oath of office on the sixteenth of Nisan." [32] However, the Hebrew prophet, who is known as Deutero-Isaiah, sneered at the priestly scientists of the Neo-Babylonian empire:

Stand fast in your enchantments and your many sorceries, with which you have labored from your youth; perhaps you may be able to succeed, perhaps you may inspire terror. You are wearied with your many counsels; let them stand forth and save you, those who divide the heavens, who gaze at the stars, who at the new moons predict what shall befall you.[33]

Despite such occasional critics, few inhabitants of the Near East doubted the powers and skills of priests and sages. In the second millennium B.C., the Canaanites had devised the alphabet, and Phoenician traders eventually spread the new device throughout the Mediterranean world. However, the literati of Egypt and Mesopotamia disdained the alphabet, possibly because they had invested a lifetime in learning the elaborate scripts and vocabularies which were the arcana of specialists.

Even in the Hellenistic era, the Palestinian sage Jeshua ben-Sirach depicted the role of intellectuals from the viewpoint of the old order:

A scribe attains wisdom through the opportunities of leisure,
And the man who has little business to do can become wise.
How can the man who holds the plow become wise,
Who glories in handling the ox-goad?
Who drives oxen and guides them at their work,
And whose discourse is with the sons of bulls?
He sets his mind on turning his furrows,
And his anxiety is about fodder for heifers. . . .
It is not so with the man who applies himself,
And studies the Law of the Most High.
He searches out the wisdom of all the ancients,
And busies himself with prophecies;
He observes the discourse of famous men,
And penetrates the intricacies of figures.
He searches out the hidden meaning of proverbs,
And acquaints himself with the obscurities of figures.
He will serve among great men,
And appear before rulers.[34]

Although the sages of the Near East were no longer an elite in the world that Alexander made, astronomy and mathematics flourished in Phoenicia into Roman times.[35] For centuries, Greek scholars had sought out Near Eastern learning and legends described pilgrimages to Egypt by Pythagoras, Anaxagoras, Democritus, and Plato.[36] In the time of Augustus, the historian Strabo visited Egypt and saw the house of Plato and the "observatory" of the astronomer Eudoxus at Heliopolis. The perceptive Strabo noted that the priests of Egypt were no longer proficient in astronomy but spent their time performing religious rites for tourists.[37]

When the Greeks attained intellectual sophistication, some Hellenes gave serious thought to the origins of science in the Near East. Dissatisfied by the theory of the pragmatic beginnings of geometry, Aristotle decided that a high science was the result of an economic surplus and leisure for the intelligentsia:

When all inventions had been discovered, the sciences which are not concerned with the pleasures and necessities of life were developed first in lands where men began to have leisure. This is the reason why mathematics originated in Egypt, for there the priestly caste was able to enjoy leisure.[38]

Although his views reflected a class bias in favor of leisure, Aristotle recognized the major role which nonpractical activity plays in the advancement of science.

The historian Diodorus Siculus contrasted the traditional methods of scientific instruction in the Near East with the intellectual anarchy of Greek education:

Because they are bred in these studies since childhood, the Chaldaeans attained great skill in them, for young people learn easily and a great amount of time is spent on study. [Many] Hellenic students of science [are superficial], . . . turn to higher subjects quite late, and . . . have to give them up when they are obliged to earn a living. Only a few, here and there, really apply themselves to higher studies and pursue them for profit, and these men always try to make some novel interpretations of the most important ideas rather than follow in the ways of their predecessors. Thus, the foreigners are competent in every detail because they always stick with the same subjects, while the Greeks with their eyes on profit are constantly founding new schools and quarreling over major problems. Since they are taught conflicting views, Greek students live in intellectual confusion and cannot place their faith in anything.[39]

Whatever Hellenistic source provided Diodorus with these insights was aware that the competitive scientists of Hellas lacked the hereditary security of their Near Eastern counterparts.

SCIENTISTS IN GREECE

Early Greek history is a morass of myths and legends, and archeology throws little light on the roles of the men in Hellas who were groping toward science. A few legends concern doctors, engineers, and inventors in the Greek Dark Ages when scientists appeared both as technicians and magicians. However, these tales have usually been preserved by Hellenistic writers who reconstructed the scientists of the remote past according to the tastes of later times.

In the second millennium B.C., the Greek peninsula was controlled by princes who built great castles at Mycenae and elsewhere. The monumental size of Mycenaean fortifications testified to the constant warfare of the age and the skill of Hellenic engineers who were able to construct great vaults and move enormous weights. Unfortunately, the Linear B documents, which have revealed many details of Mycenaean society, supply no information about early Greek builders. About 1100 B.C., Hellas succumbed to Dorian invaders, who blanketed the land with barbarism and illiteracy. In the eighth century, writing returned to Greece when Phoenician traders introduced the alphabet. About the same time, the Homeric poems preserved the traditions of the blood-stained Dark Ages and reflected the social values of Greeks who lived on the coast of Asia Minor.

In an era of continuous war, doctors were appreciated as leeches if not as scientists. In the *Iliad,* the physician Machaon was wounded before the walls of Troy and was carefully carried from the battlefield, for "a surgeon who can cut out an arrow and heal a wound with salves is worth many men." [40] Machaon later treated the injuries of King Menelaus with ointments that his father, Asclepius, had supposedly received from the centaur Chiron. [41] Whether Asclepius was originally a deified doctor or a healing deity is of less significance than the conviction of later generations that the god of medicine was a great physician who had been elevated, like Imhotep, to divine status. [42] According to Diodorus Siculus, Asclepius was deified for his work with surgery, drugs, and herbs. [43] Cicero believed that the mythical Asclepius evolved from traditions of two medical pioneers—one invented probes and splints, and the other was the first man to extract teeth and employ purgatives. [44] To most Greeks, Asclepius was unquestionably a god, who was the patron of doctors and healed believers by appearing to them in dreams. He was also the holy serpent which was kept in his temples. However, Hellenistic rationalists saw Asclepius primarily as the memory of a medical pioneer.

By the eighth century B.C., much of Greece had emerged from the barbarism of the Dark Ages, but life was fairly crude in rural areas. In many parts of the Mediterranean, Greek colonists lived in proximity to barbarians and even savages. Consequently, Hellenes venerated inventors as heroes who had created the essentials of civilization. The simplest discoveries and improvements in technology separated the Greeks from tattooed barbarians who rinsed their mouths with urine and bartered captives for jugs of wine.⁴⁵ The Celts of Gaul, for example, nailed the heads of dead enemies to lodge poles, the Scythians of the Ukraine took scalps, and the Cimbri of Northern Europe divined the future in the entrails of dying men.⁴⁶ Early Greek science must be viewed as the activity of men of curiosity and inventiveness who often dwelt, like Franklin and Jefferson, within a few days' ride of primitive savages. To the Greeks, the deification of inventors was a meaningful concept. However, Hellenistic rationalists obscured the history of science by spying a dead genius behind every hero or god.⁴⁷ According to Polybius, Danaus was rewarded with kingship rather than divinity for introducing reservoirs in Argos, and a similar honor was bestowed on Atreus, who discovered that the motion of the sun was contrary to that of the stars.⁴⁸ Diodorus Siculus even claimed that the legendary giant Atlas had been an African king who perfected astrology and developed the doctrine of celestial spheres.⁴⁹ Thus, Hercules taking the heavens from Atlas' back was an allegory of the transmission of astrology to mankind by Hercules.⁵⁰ Diodorus' whimsies are as worthless as the theory of the historian Ephorus who believed that the Scythian sage Anacharsis invented the bellows, the two-fluked anchor, and the potter's wheel. The historian Strabo easily refuted Ephorus by pointing out that the potter's wheel was mentioned in the Homeric poems long before Anacharsis, who was a contemporary of Solon.⁵¹ In the dawn of history, most inventions were devised by anonymous craftsmen or evolved from the secret lore of guilds, but rarely was mankind indebted to the inventive genius of a renowned sage.

While most tales of early inventors deserve little credence, the legend of Daedalus presents a unique problem. During the Dark Ages the Greeks told stories of an Athenian architect and inventor, Daedalus, who had found employment in Minoan Crete. In Homer's words, Daedalus "built a dancing-floor at Knossos for fair-haired Ariadne." ⁵² To later writers, the Athenian technician had also fashioned statues so lifelike that they seemed to walk around.⁵³ The connection of Daedalus with the "Daedalic" sculptures of the eighth and seventh century was anachronistic. Nevertheless, a detailed life of Daedalus took form: the great inventor became jealous and murdered his assistant Talos, who had devised an iron saw and a drawing compass. The act of violence explained Daedalus' flight from Athens to Crete, where a technician would be welcome even if he was escaping from justice. At Knossos, Daedalus served King Minos and his daughter Ariadne but eventually lost favor at court. The inventor fled with his son Icarus to Sicily, where he constructed reservoirs and steam baths for King Cocalus. When Minos came in pursuit of Daedalus, the Cretan monarch was lured to his death in the baths.[54] Behind this farrago may lie memories of a Minoan settlement in Sicily, but not much history can be sifted from the tale. Greek moralists embroidered Daedalus' flight from Crete with the episode of Icarus, who flew on artificial wings but disregarded his father's instructions and plunged to his death in the sea. Although the adventures of Daedalus belong to fiction and folklore, archeology has substantiated the equally implausible legends of Troy and Minoan Crete. In the great palace at Knossos, a Linear B tablet recorded a dedication of holy oil "to Daidaleion," apparently a hero cult of the famed inventor.[55] While the details of his life do not warrant much belief, the name of Daedalus is probably a valid memory of an actual Bronze Age craftsman who was skilled in many things and served in the palace at Knossos.

A vague figure from the mythical era of Greek prehistory was the titan Prometheus. At the beginning of the seventh century B.C., the poet Hesiod identified Prometheus as the benefactor who had taught men to use fire,[56] but by the fifth century, the dramatist Aeschylus claimed that "Prometheus had founded all the arts of mankind." [57] As the fire-bringer, Prometheus was a Greek version of the Indian deity Pramantha who was the personification of the fire-making drill. Angry over Prometheus' service to mankind, Zeus condemned the titan to savage tortures.[58] The plight of Prometheus dramatized Hesiod's contention that justice was notably absent on earth and in heaven, but the titan's martyrdom was a moral parable and not a relic in the history of science.

In the middle of the sixth century B.C., the plausible episode of Phalaris and Perilaüs took place. Like Daedalus, Perilaüs was an Athenian technician who found employment in Sicily. A sculptor and bronze-worker, Perilaüs devised and built a bronze bull for the famous tyrant Phalaris of Acragas.[59] Although in general a brutal ruler, Phalaris occasionally acted with generosity and even freed would-be assassins.[60] When the inventor revealed that the bronze bull roared when men were roasted in its interior, the outraged despot placed Perilaüs in the terrible contrivance, removed him half-dead so as not to pollute the statue, and had him thrown from a cliff.[61] Although the bull had been ordered as a religious image, legends soon depicted Phalaris as an ogre who had roasted men in a bronze bull. While the existence of the bull has been accepted by many historians,[62] the relation between its inventor and the tyrant has received little attention. The punishment of Perilaüs may only be a Hellenistic parable, but the tale reflects a neat sense of the responsibility of inventors for their products.

During the sixth century B.C., Greeks in Italy and Asia Minor laid the foundations for a true science in Hellas. While the gods were not abandoned, supernatural explanations were no longer considered adequate for most phenomena. With effort and imagination, Greek thinkers tried to comprehend the material world but were handicapped by the rudimentary nature of their scientific methods. Regrettably for the peoples of antiquity, the intellectual conquest of the natural world was very limited. Although the combustibility of oil and coal was well known, fossil fuels were not utilized in the service of man. Ancient society continued to exploit the muscle power of humans and animals. Like the Egyptians, the Greeks and Romans developed mechanics into a science in order to help men and beasts move matter. Although many men were interested in the pragmatic application of science, the composition of matter troubled only a handful of thinkers, who tried to determine the ways of nature without accurate means of measurement. While they did not effect an industrial revolution, the pre-Socratic scientists achieved an intellectual breakthrough and replaced myths with explanations that were subject to definition, argument, and the rules of evidence.

Although often heralded as an expression of "the Greek miracle," the rise of scientific thought in Greece was complex in origin. In the seventh and sixth century, the Greek cities experienced a breakdown in traditional values which accompanied the evolution of a money economy. In the market place, the kin-based ethics of clansmen were strained by the profit motive which pitted individual interests against family obligations. As venerable family ties were supplanted by property values, newly rich plutocrats replaced blooded aristocrats in positions of political power. Noble families survived by intermarriage with the commercial class. As the two classes blended, it became evident that there were at least two sides to most questions. In search of trade and land, Greeks went abroad and observed the ways of other men. Exposure to alien cultures and climes often had a disquieting effect on parochial-minded Hellenic travelers, who were awed by the variety of customs and the relativity of mores in strange lands. In the Near East, Greeks were in contact with advanced societies, and some wished to learn the wisdom of the high civilizations of Asia and Africa. In time, Hellenic thought would surpass its mentors.

The great political fact of the sixth century was the extension of the Persian empire from the Indus Valley to Libya in Africa and Macedon in Europe. With his usual zest, Herodotus recounted a parable of Hellenic envoys at the court of Darius the Great. To shame the parochialism of the Greeks, the king pointed out the divergent burial customs throughout his vast empire and illustrated the hold of convention on mankind.[63] The setting of the story was significant—the court of the king of the world, through whose domains all men could travel in safety and return with full pockets and open minds. Within the universal state of Persia, local customs were subordinate to a universal law, the law of the Medes and the Persians. A few Greek thinkers mused that there might also be a natural law to which all things must conform. The awareness of relativity had discredited old traditions, but the fervent search for natural law often bred new myths.

Happily for the speculators of the sixth century, Greece did not support a sacerdotal establishment that insisted upon orthodox religious beliefs. Formal religion among the Greeks was secular, and piety was demonstrated by public attendance at the rites of the gods. Pious men were always careful to sacrifice to the gods, but the priests did not inquire about the particulars of their views of the divine. At Delphi, the oracle was indifferent to heterodoxy, for gold, not conformity, was the consuming passion of the priests of Apollo.[64] Greek science did not have to face the hostility of a priestly vested interest, nor did it acquire a sacerdotal tone. Although they studied the lore of the Near East with amateur enthusiasm, the emerging scientists of Greece did not imitate the mentality of Near Eastern priests who venerated habit and had a horror of change. Being free men, Greek intellectuals had their own flaws—they took pride in small accomplishments and tended to view themselves as an elite.

From the viewpoint of puritans and Platonists, a sage must be nothing less than a saint. The first Greek intellectuals were too crass for Plato's taste, for the early intelligentsia of Ionia and Italy had been men of affairs who often dabbled in business. As an antidote to the rude realities of history, the Platonic Academy assembled a golden legend about the unworldly pre-Socratics and represented them as philosophic saints and absentminded professors.[65] In typical tales, Thales tumbled into a ditch because he was lost in contemplation of the stars, and Democritus was outfoxed by his worldly brothers and spent his inheritance on travel and education.[66] When Darius asked Heraclitus to his court, the philosopher rebuffed the invitation of the king: "I am content with little when that little is my own mind." [67] Heraclitus' rejection of Persian patronage was an early version of the tableau of the Sage and the King which is redundant in the history of ideas.*

More plausible traditions record efforts by philosophers and scientists to secure the patronage of princes and cities. The willingness of powerful men and states to attract and honor famous thinkers was not due to altruism. The presence of noted sages was both ornamental and useful. The philosopher Anaximander supplied his patrons with gnomons and maps, and engineers flocked to the court of Polycrates, the sixth-century tyrant of Samos.[68] The achievements of Polycrates' engineers impressed Herodotus a century later:

They built three of the greatest constructions in Hellas. One was a tunnel running straight through the base of a 900 foot high hill. The
* Invariably, the sage got the best of the conversation, for behind the tableau lay the mythic confrontation of the God and the King, which Euripides immortalized in the *Bacchae* and the Gospel of John depicted in the court of Pilate.

length of the tunnel is almost a mile, and the height and width are each eight feet. Along the course of the tunnel there is another cutting, thirty feet deep and three feet wide, through which spring water is piped into the city. The tunnel was designed by Eupalinus of Megara. . . . The next great work was a breakwater which protects the harbor and is nearly 120 feet deep and 400 yards long. The third construction was a temple [for Hera] which is the largest temple known. The architect was Rhoecus of Samos.[69]

Like the despots of Renaissance Italy, Polycrates of Samos employed skilled technicians to enhance the beauty and comfort of his city. However, Darius used Samian engineers for other purposes. When the king invaded the Balkans, Mandrocles of Samos built a pontoon bridge on which Persian troops crossed the Bosporus. A generation later, the Greek engineer Harpalus constructed a similar bridge over the Hellespont for Xerxes' ill-fated expedition against Greece.[70]

In the Ionian cities of Greek Asia, the philosopher Thales pioneered in science and meddled in politics. His scientific reputation in Ionia was so great that gullible men credited Thales with predicting the eclipse of 585 B.C.[71] A member of a prominent family in Miletus, Thales was active in politics and may have been an associate of the tyrant Thrasybulus.[72] According to Herodotus, Thales served the Lydian king Alyattes as an astronomer and was employed by his successor Croesus as an engineer.[73] If Thales worked for Alyattes, the scientist was quite elderly when he advised the Milesians to stay aloof from Croesus' war with Cyrus of Persia.[74] Herodotus also reports that Thales proposed a federation of Ionian cities with a capital at Teos, but it is not clear whether the union was aimed against Lydia or Persia.[75] When the Ionian cities plotted to rise against Darius in 500 B.C., the geographer Hecataeus counseled restraint, for he knew the great extent and resources of the Persian empire.[76] Later, Hecataeus prepared a map of the world for the rebel leader Aristagoras who was seeking aid from King Cleomenes of Sparta. Unwittingly, the Ionian politician frightened the Spartan king who had no idea that Persia or the world was so large.[77] Because Hecataeus was too honest a cartographer, his map caused Cleomenes to refuse aid to the Ionians in their revolt.

In the sixth century B.C., doctors were as much in demand as nuclear scientists are today. The medical school at Croton in Italy produced Democedes who earned impressive fees as a public physician at Aegina and Athens. At Samos, the doctor was paid the enormous sum of two talents by the tyrant Polycrates. When Samos fell to the Persians, Democedes joined the court of Darius and won the king's respect by curing him of a sprain after Egyptian doctors had failed. As the royal physician, Democedes successfully treated Queen Atossa for an abscess of the breast. Through Atossa's influence, the doctor received a commission to visit the West on an espionage mission for Darius. Although the king sent an escort to insure Democedes' return, the wily physician eluded his guards and returned home to Croton. The city refused to hand over its distinguished doctor to Darius' envoys, and Democedes soon married the daughter of the famous athlete Milo.[78] While the career of Democedes at Aegina, Athens, and Samos is proof of his medical ability and justifies the fame of Crotonite medicine, his adventure with Darius also demonstrates the worldly wisdom of the great physician.

Ironically, little is known of the life of Hippocrates, the alleged "father of medicine." [79] Apparently he was a fifth-century physician who accepted money from patients and taught medicine on the island of Cos. To fourth-century writers, Hippocrates was famous enough to serve as an example of a distinguished doctor.[80] There is no connection between Hippocrates and the miscalled "Hippocratic Oath," which was not even representative of Greek medical practice. The Oath prohibited doctors from performing surgery, inducing abortions, and assisting patients to commit suicide, but Hellenic society had no objection to such activities, nor did most Greek physicians. Probably, the document was a manifesto of Pythagorean medical reformers in the fourth century.[81] Hippocratic doctors were less squeamish and more concerned with medicine than with morality; their professional ethics were high, and their skills were soundly based in practice and the study of case histories. Medical education flourished on Cos and on the nearby island of Cnidus, for able doctors found ready employment in the disease-ridden ancient world. Ctesias of Cnidus was court physician to Darius II and Artaxerxes II and tended the wounds of the latter after the battle of Cunaxa.[82] After seventeen years at the lively Persian court,

Ctesias turned his talents to diplomacy and served as a lobbyist for Evagoras, the tyrant of Cyprus. In 397, Ctesias represented Persia on a mission to Sparta but returned to Cnidus, where he devoted the rest of his life to writing gossipy accounts of recent history and fabulous tales of the East. He was probably a better physician than he was a historian.

The career of Ctesias' contemporary, Eudoxus of Cnidus, illustrates the opportunities that were available to scientists in the fourth century. Although he was most famous for his theory of concentric planetary spheres,[83] Eudoxus did not limit his studies to astronomy but also served as a physician. After studying mathematics in Italy and medicine in Sicily, Eudoxus visited Athens and went on to Egypt with a letter of introduction from King Agesilaus of Sparta to the Pharaoh Nectanebo. For sixteen months "with beard and eyebrows shaved," Eudoxus studied with the priests of Egypt. Returning to Athens, the versatile scientist provoked the anger of Plato by advocating a life of restrained hedonism. After serving at the court of Mausolus of Caria, Eudoxus retired to Cnidus where he drew up laws for his fellow citizens.[84] While some of the details of his life are doubtful, the substance of Eudoxus' career is probable enough.

The most famous scientist of the fourth century was Aristotle. His father Nicomachus had been the court physician of King Amyntas of Macedon and claimed descent from Machaon and Asclepius.[85] A successful and wealthy doctor, Nicomachus provided an excellent education for Aristotle. After his father's death, the boy was sent to Athens to study under Plato. While he was awed by the personality of Plato, Aristotle never forgot the practical wisdom of Nicomachus, who must have impressed upon his son the advantages of patronage. At the Academy in Athens, Aristotle became a close friend of Plato and hoped to succeed him as director of the institution. However, the older philosopher chose as his successor a relative, Speusippus. Thwarted in his academic career, Aristotle and a few friends withdrew from the Academy and sought the patronage of the tyrant Hermias in Asia Minor. Aristotle married the tyrant's niece and later defended his memory when Hermias was crucified by his Persian overlords.[86] Before Hermias' downfall, Aristotle had moved to Lesbos and then to Macedon. The practical

Aristotle hoped to be a close adviser to Philip who was the most powerful ruler in the Greek world.

At the Macedonian court, Aristotle was appointed tutor of the crown prince Alexander. The philosopher advised the future king to consider Asiatics an inferior breed who were designed by nature to serve as slaves. However, Alexander later realized that Asia could not be ruled with the mentality of a "pukka sahib." Various anecdotes record the estrangement of the world conqueror from his former tutor, whose nephew Callisthenes served as Alexander's propaganda chief but was executed for conspiring against the young king.[87] While Alexander was engaged in the conquest of the Persian empire, Aristotle was in Athens, where he established the Lyceum as a rival school to the Academy. Despite the strained relations between Aristotle and Alexander, the philosopher was a personal friend of Antipater, the Macedonian viceroy. Consequently, Aristotle was considered pro-Macedonian by the Athenians. In 323, the news of Alexander's death reached Athens and Aristotle had to flee to nearby Chalcis.[88] When Greek nationalists canceled the honorary decree which he had received at Delphi for chronological research, Aristotle wrote to Antipater: "About the voting at Delphi which deprived me of my honors, I feel that I am sorry but not much."[89] Within a year the philosopher died despondent and left Antipater as executor of his will.[90]

Although his life ended in exile, Aristotle had profited from Macedonian generosity and established a research institute at the Lyceum. His students studied subjects as varied as the structure of sea animals and the political institutions of Carthage. Werner Jaeger has hailed Aristotle as "the first person to investigate the sensible as the vehicle of the universal."[91] In the development of scientific method, Aristotle's enthusiasm for laboratory work was a great improvement over the mathematical orientation of Plato's Academy. Aristotle ordered his students to investigate the material world before worrying about natural law:

We therefore must not recoil with childish aversion from the examination of the humbler animals. Every realm of nature is marvelous: and as Heraclitus, when the strangers who came to visit him found him warming himself at the furnace in the kitchen and hesitated to go in, is reported to have bidden them not to be afraid to enter, as even in that kitchen divinities were present, so we should venture on the study of every kind of animal without distaste; for each and all will reveal to us something natural and something beautiful. Absence of haphazard and conduciveness of everything to an end are to be found in Nature's works in the highest degree, and the resultant end of her generations and combinations is a form of the beautiful.[92]

Despite the teleological trend of Aristotle's thought, readers may be reminded of the lyrical description of evolving nature with which Charles Darwin concluded *The Origin of the Species.*[93]

Regrettably, Aristotle's scientific élan did not insure an objective approach to the issue of racial differences. Like most of his contemporaries, the philosopher believed in the racial superiority of Greeks and their natural right to conquer and rule "barbarians" or non-Greeks. But this had not always been the "Hellenic point of view." In the *Iliad,* the Asiatic Trojans were portrayed with sympathy, and the word *barbaros* was not used to describe non-Hellenes [94]—the word itself was a later slur on the speech of foreigners which seemed a babble to ignorant Greeks. In the fifth century, the dramatist Aeschylus celebrated the success of Greek resistance to Persian aggression, but he treated the enemy with respect and had no notions that they were racially inferior. Herodotus used the term "barbarian" for non-Greeks, but he admired the civilized nations of the Near East. As for the Persians, the historian noted that, at the battle of Plataea, "the barbarians seized the Greek spears and snapped them, for the Persians are not inferior to Greeks in courage or strength." [95] In Hellas, most slaves were foreigners, and some Greeks equated barbarian birth with servile status. In Sophocles' *Ajax,* King Agamemnon mocked the barbaric speech of Teucer, but the slave defied the Greek and boasted of his own service with the heroic Ajax:

> Beside him stood
> I, the slave, the barbarian mother's son.
> Wretch, with what face can you fling forth such taunts?
> Know you not that of old your father's father
> Was Pelops, a barbarian and a Phrygian? [96]

Thucydides, who was part Thracian, also emphasized that the Greeks had only recently emerged from real barbarism.[97] Hippias of Elis insisted that all men were brothers by nature and only foolishly divided by custom,[98] and another sophist, Antiphon, scoffed at artificial distinctions between Greeks and barbarians, since all men have the same bodies and breathe the same air.[99] A fifth-century medical tract, *Airs, Waters, and Places,* ascribed the differences between men to climatic factors but added a significant qualification: "Even if he is born naturally brave and spirited, a man is changed by the laws. . . . All the peoples of Asia—Greek or barbarian—who are independent and free from despots, toil for themselves and are the most warlike of men." [100] Not all Hellenes were so generous—in his old age, the poet Euripides defended the right of Greeks to rule over barbarians on the premise that "they are slaves." [101] The Spartans won the Peloponnesian War with Persian subsidies, but the attitude toward non-Greeks shifted radically in the fourth century when Persia was in decline. Spartan imperialists promoted the myth that Asiatics were racially inferior, because "contempt for the enemy instills strength in battle"—King Agesilaus of Sparta stripped captured Asians to show that foreigners were "white-skinned and soft-muscled, for they never stripped in the sun and always rode." [102] Aristotle's mentor, Plato, believed in racial characteristics and a natural enmity between Greeks and barbarians.[103] The contemporary educator, Isocrates, conceded that culture, not racial differences, separated mankind, but he served the interests of Philip of Macedon and called loudly for a Greek attack on Persia to enslave the peoples of the East.[104] In the jingoistic atmosphere of the times, it is understandable but still regrettable that Aristotle did not transcend the new racial doctrines of Hellas.

Teleology was easily adapted to sanctify imperialism and justify Greek domination of Asian peoples whom nature had presumably intended to be slaves. In the *Politics,* Aristotle advocated a frank racism:

The peoples of cold countries generally, and particularly those of Europe, are full of spirit but deficient in skill and intelligence; and this is why they continue to remain comparatively free, but attain no political development and show no capacity for governing others. The peoples of Asia are endowed with skill and intelligence but are deficient in spirit, and this is why they continue to be peoples of subjects and slaves. The Greek stock, intermediate in geographical position, unites the qualities of both sets of peoples. It possesses both spirit and intelligence: the one quality makes it continue free; the other enables it to attain the highest political development and to show a capacity for governing every other people—if only it could once achieve political unity.[105]

In 338, Philip had taken the first step toward the unification of Greece by establishing the Hellenic League to support his war to enslave Asia. Under his successor Alexander, the Greek states were restless and Aristotle apparently composed his remarks on racial superiority and Hellenic unity for the benefit of the new king. While the Greeks fretted under Macedonian control, the "barbarians" of Italy were achieving remarkable political success as the Roman Republic extended citizenship to many cities in central Italy. Aristotle had heard of Rome and was well aware that all Europeans were not savages.[106] He also knew that many Asians were free and spirited, and he even praised the political institutions and stability of the Semitic state of Carthage in North Africa.[107] However, "scientific" racism required selective facts and sweeping generalities, and Aristotle callously advised Alexander to consider non-Greeks as "animals and plants." [108] With the Aristotelean insistence upon empirical investigation, Hellenic science had come of age, but Aristotle's preaching of racism revealed a serious weakness in the greatest of Greek scientists. Fortunately for the peoples of Asia, Alexander paid no attention to Aristotle when he formulated policy in the conquered areas.

GREEK SCIENCE AND POLITICS

The relationship of scientists to Greek city states was complicated by the fact that some scientists thought that an intellectual elite ought to exercise political authority. From Plato to H. G. Wells, many moralists have advocated rule by philosophers and/or scientists. Practical politicians have been less enthusiastic and raised the objection that scholars are impractical theorists. In practice, most mandarins have been efficient rulers, and many men of action have been as unrealistic as cloistered monks. In the Hellenic world, scientists often served as public figures and the Pythagoreans even ruled communities in southern Italy.

In the cities of Sicily and Italy, the scientist as ruler often appeared in an aura of magic, which was fostered to impress the masses and became the basis for pious legends. Both Empedocles and Pythagoras indulged in miracle mongering and exploited the devotion of their disciples. The lives of the two great scientists became so encrusted with legendary feats that it is difficult to separate fact from fiction. In fifth-century Sicily, Empedocles announced his own divinity after raising a woman from a thirty-day trance. At Selinus, he accepted divine honors for his public health measures, which halted an epidemic and improved the water supply of the city.[109] A wealthy and influential citizen of Acragas, Empedocles led the democratic faction and broke the hold of oligarchs on the machinery of local government.[110] A careful observer of physical phenomena,[111] Empedocles used his knowledge of science to impress his fellow citizens and win their political support.

In Italy, Pythagoreans dominated many Greek cities at the end of the sixth century. In 530, Pythagoras had arrived in Croton as a refugee from the tyranny of Polycrates on Samos.[112] Charming and persuasive, the great mathematician was soon a political force in the city and his followers dominated the civic life of Croton.[113] The Pythagorean political clubs were monopolized by individuals who were more interested in politics than in science. More sincere Pythagoreans embraced a quasi-monastic discipline and shared property in common. Like Catholic monks and Chinese thought reformers, the Pythagoreans achieved sodality by severe indoctrination and enforced silence in the early stages of training. At the feet of the Master, the disciples studied mathematics and astronomy and hoped to achieve personal immortality.[114] Although Pythagorean hagiographers composed fantastic gospels which buried the actual achievements of Pythagoras in wondrous nonsense, a fairly sound tradition suggests that the charismatic philosopher was truly "a combination of Einstein and Mrs. Eddy." [115] The Greeks did not regard science and religion as incompatible, and almost all ancient thinkers hoped for divine inspiration. The members of the Pythagorean brotherhood were teetotaling vegetarians and famed for their devotion to the order and to each other. The tale of Damon and Pythias was a Pythagorean parable which became part of the folklore of Europe.[116] A pious tradition described the martyrdom of Pythagoras in an uprising led by a rejected admirer, but the episode is unlikely since the Pythagoreans continued to hold power after the death of the Master.

At Croton a group of 300 Pythagoreans controlled the city, and similar Pythagorean lodges dominated other towns in southern Italy.[117] Officially, the brotherhood prohibited the eating of beans because they believed that beans contained the souls of the dead. However, Aristotle suggests that the ban may have had a political corollary, for the Greeks often used beans in selections by lot.[118] Details of the Pythagorean regimes must be treated with some skepticism. At Locri, the Pythagorean Zaleucus required religious belief and moral behavior from the citizenry but permitted ladies of easy virtue to dress in bright colors.[119] However, puritanic lawgivers rarely display such a sense of humor. At Thurii, another Pythagorean, Charondas, devised an effective deterrent against unnecessary legislation. Thurian politicians proposed new laws with their necks in nooses to facilitate their immediate hanging if the motion failed—only three hardy citizens had the stamina to propose legislation.[120] Unfortunately, Charondas is a hazy figure who probably lived much earlier in the city of Catana, and, according to Aristotle, his laws were precise but not novel.[121] Hellenistic scholars insisted that Charondas established public schools, but the tale was a projection of an educational ideal into the remote past.[122]

The legend of Pythagorean concern for general education probably grew out of an awareness that the brotherhood had a high regard for public health and the study of medicine. Charondas was supposed to have argued that schools were a reasonable expenditure for cities which invested in public physicians.[123] Athens and most Hellenic states hired public doctors, but no Greek city provided free medical care for its inhabitants. Governmental responsibility for public health ended with efforts to lure prominent doctors to the city with guarantees of high fees and perhaps a cash bonus for the initial move. According to the leading authority on the subject, "a public physician was generally nothing more than a doctor whose fixed residence was guaranteed for a specified period." [124] In major emergencies or for an interesting case, some physicians offered their services without charge, but no Greek state established a National Health Service. Although state effort was sometimes expended in relief work, the Greeks were notoriously indifferent to the educational and medical responsibilities of government.

While they did not legislate for public medicine, the Pythagoreans were dedicated to the ideal of health in the individual. Croton was a Mecca for food faddists and medical students, and the Olympic athlete Milo was as renowned as his friend Pythagoras.[125] The city boasted a great medical school which had produced Democedes and later the Pythagorean Alcmaeon; the latter discovered the optic nerve and believed that the brain was the controlling organ of the body.[126] Insisting that science depended on empirical evidence, Alcmaeon qualified Pythagorean dogmatism by emphasizing the role that chance plays in nature.[127] Borrowing a metaphor from politics, Alcmaeon observed: "Health is the equal balance of wet and dry, hot and cold, bitter and sweet, and the rest, but the monarchy of any of them causes disease." [128] Unfortunately, the balance that Alcmaeon identified as health in the body was absent in the political life of the cities which were dominated by the Pythagorean clubs.

Regardless of their scientific achievements, the Pythagorean regimes in southern Italy degenerated into oppressive oligarchies. Even in the time of Pythagoras, Croton had waged a holy war against the rival city of Sybaris, destroyed the ancient town, and massacred its inhabitants. To later generations, the rule of the Pythagorean elect served as a glaring example of the abuse of power by intellectuals in office.[129] About 454, violent revolutions broke out in the Italian cities and the brotherhood was overthrown. Everywhere, Pythagorean buildings were destroyed and many members were slain. At Tarentum, some Pythagoreans were burned alive by irate mobs.[130] According to the historian Polybius, the liberated Italian cities eventually adopted the democratic institutions of mainland Greece.[131] After the purges, surviving Pythagoreans concentrated on the study of science and philosophy—activities which were more compatible with the

ideals of Pythagoras. The political debacle of the Pythagorean
clubs spared Greek mathematics from developing as the cult
secret of a scientific hierarchy.

Although the days of Pythagorean rule had ended, individual
Pythagoreans pursued successful careers in the late fifth and
early fourth century. The Pythagorean Philolaus won fame as
the creator of a planetary system in which the earth moved about
a central fire.[132] Supposedly, the astronomer published the secret
doctrines of Pythagoras and sold some of the Master's treatises
to Plato.[133] According to Diogenes Laertius, Philolaus died trying
to establish a tyranny in his native city of Croton.[134] At Tarentum, the Pythagorean Archytas was a prominent politician and
exerted influence to rescue Plato when the Athenian philosopher
was in danger at Syracuse.[135] When not involved in politics,
Archytas invented mechanical gadgets and automata, taught
geometry to Eudoxus, and investigated the mathematical problems of the cube.[136] According to an apocryphal epistle, Plato
was worried that Archytas might desert politics for the pleasures
of science:

You think it a heavy trial not to be able to get free from the cares
of public life. It is indeed one of the sweetest things in life to follow
one's own interests, especially when they are such as you have chosen;
practically everyone would agree. But this also you must bear in
mind, that none of us is born for himself alone; a part of our existence belongs to our country, a part to our parents, a part to our
friends, and a large part is given to the circumstances that command
our lives. When our country calls us to public service, it would, I
think, be unnatural to refuse; especially since this means giving place
to unworthy men who enter public life for motives other than the
best.[137] *

Although Archytas did not need encouragement to continue the
pursuit of power, the tone of the letter is consistent with the
Platonic view that politics has priority over pure science.

In the history of ideas, Plato presents an interesting problem.
Because his writings are accepted as classics and have intrinsic

* From *Plato's Epistles*, translated by Glenn R. Morrow, copyright (c) 1962
by the Bobbs-Merrill Company, reprinted by permission of the publishers.

worth, Plato has acquired a posthumous following of disciples who cherish his memory as they conceive it. Similarly, the philosopher has been the target of opponents whose quarrel is more often with Platonists than with Plato. While enthusiasts hail him as a precursor of either Christianity or Marxism, critics sneer that Plato was a political reactionary and a homosexual snob.[138] In his views on democracy and sex, Plato was conditioned by the aristocratic circles of late fifth-century Athens. Although undoubtedly influenced by Pythagorean thought, his authoritarian concepts of science and politics warrant attention.

In the aftermath of the Peloponnesian War, Athens suffered under a reactionary oligarchy which was led by Plato's kinsmen. When democracy was restored, Plato was disenchanted with the old aristocracy because his relatives had ruled with cruelty and terror. Like many men in similar straits, Plato turned to intellectual pursuits and found salvation in the study of mathematics, which seemed to reveal a supermundane world of eternal absolutes. However, Plato never lost his zest for politics and eagerly accepted an invitation from Dionysius I of Syracuse to grace the tyrant's court. Plato hoped to be an adviser to the despot and did form a close friendship with Dionysius' brother in law, Dion. However Plato and the tyrant soon quarreled, for Dionysius did not relish advice from a philosopher and Plato took no pleasure in a courtier's role. When Plato left Syracuse to return to Athens, Dionysius ordered the ship captain to sell the philosopher as a slave, but Plato was quickly ransomed by his friends.[139] At Athens, Plato established the Academy as an institute for advanced studies in mathematics and philosophy. In many respects, the Academy was a secular version of the Pythagorean community at Croton, for Plato provided a sound education in mathematics and encouraged his pupils to engage in political action.

Although a philosophic mystic, Plato was an activist in politics and believed that intellectual elites should rule cities. Plato returned to Syracuse to serve briefly as a philosophic counselor to Dionysius II. However, the young tyrant soon suspected that the philosopher was an agent of his uncle Dion, who was prominent in the new government. Shortly after the philosopher left Sicily, Dionysius drove Dion into exile where he plotted with

Plato's friends to seize power at Syracuse. On a final mission to Sicily, Plato tried to reconcile Dionysius with Dion, but the negotiations collapsed and Plato only escaped through the intercession of Archytas of Tarentum. When Dion decided to employ force, members of the Academy sailed with his expedition against Syracuse.[140] Although he easily overthrew Dionysius, Dion was soon involved in a bloody power struggle with the democrats in the city. In overcoming his opponents, Dion became a brutal despot. Within a few years he was assassinated by a member of the Academy, Callippus, who set himself up as tyrant.[141] The disastrous involvement of the Academy with Dion discouraged Plato from further political adventures, but some of his disciples still preferred political action to theory.[142] At Lampsacus, for example, the Platonist Euaeon tried to foreclose a mortgage on the acropolis, but the citizens repaid the debt and expelled the man who had hoped to seize their citadel and rule the city.[143] In the third century two members of the Academy, Ecdemus and Megalophanes, helped to overthrow tyrants at Sicyon and Megalopolis and restored order in the strife-torn city of Cyrene.[144] With the exception of Ecdemus and Megalophanes, most of the excursions of the Academy into politics were as abortive as those of the Pythagorean brotherhood.

Fortunately, no Greek city was subjected to a truly Platonic regime, for Syracuse only replaced one tyrant with another when Dion ousted Dionysius II. Life in a Platonic city would have been grim and regimented; books were to be licensed and science controlled by the state. Plato approved of the persecution of the astronomer Anaxagoras at Athens and hoped that the books of Democritus would be seized and burned.[145] According to Plato, Homer and Hesiod lied about the gods and should not be read by the young.[146] In his old age, Plato outlined a practical theocracy in his dialogue *The Laws,* and recommended the establishment of an astral religion with severe measures to enforce belief in the divinity of heavenly bodies. The well-ordered state could not tolerate the blasphemous notion that the planets wandered from perfect circular orbits.[147] Adherents of "atheistical astronomy" would be arrested and confined in reeducation centers, where infidels who remained incorrigible after five years would be executed.[148] In the words of E. R. Dodds, "the nearest historical analogue is not the Inquisition, but those trials of 'intellectual deviationists' with which our own generation has become so familiar." [149] To Plato, astronomy was always secondary to the intuitive insights of his philosophy.

In their attempts to achieve a high science, Greek intellectuals were handicapped by the social conventions of Hellas. Although social and economic changes had raised the status of the commercial and working classes, the overwhelming majority of Greek intellectuals were members of a leisure class who reflected the views of a defunct aristocracy and disdained labor and commerce. Such values were obsolete relics of the aristocratic society that had dominated Greece before the sixth century. To the detriment of the development of science, the medical profession was divided into leeches and physicians, that is, common practitioners and learned theorists. [150] Yet even Plato admitted that slave doctors cured their patients while gentlemen physicians were often more interested in the nature of disease than in effecting cures. [151] In the Hellenistic age, the historian Polybius repeated the charge that theory-oriented doctors were woefully inadequate. [152] In practice, army doctors and witches saved many patients who would have died in the inept hands of a medical scholar. Nevertheless, the class bias of Hellas honored the educated theorist and despised the skillful surgeon.

With the exception of the commercial Corinthians, the leaders of Greek society had a low opinion of banausoi or men who worked for a living. [153] Bankers, businessmen, and most doctors were considered banausoi. Aristotle felt that it was in poor taste even to discuss most banausic professions. [154] He also believed that banausoi could not fulfill civic duties because their energies were consumed by lowly affairs. [155] The classic expression of contempt for the banausic occupations was made by the Athenian squire Xenophon:

The banausic trades spoil the bodies of workers and foremen who are forced to sit still and work indoors. They often spend the whole day at the fire. The debilitation of the body is accompanied by a serious weakening of the mind. Moreover, the banausic occupations leave no spare time for service to one's friends or the city. Thus, the banausoi are considered unreliable friends and poor defenders of their country. [156]

Xenophon praised Sparta for prohibiting the banausic arts to its citizens. He also endorsed the view of the Persian kings that only agriculture and war were respectable. Ironically, the Greeks would one day adopt the cult of a crucified carpenter preached by a tentmaker.

Hellenic contempt for labor was related to the social acceptance of slavery. Although most Greeks did not own slaves, the masses envied the great slave owners and aped their ideology.[156a] Xenophon described an impoverished freeman who was willing to perform manual labor rather than accept a position as an estate manager, because such jobs were usually held by executive slaves who were accustomed to servility.[157] The ever present spectacle of slavery and the grinding poverty of the masses reinforced the distinction between the leisure class and all those who, free or slave, labored for a living. Education, too, instilled even in the middle class an awe for cerebral activity and a disdain for physical labor. Recently, Bertrand Gille has challenged this view:

The disdain of technical problems evinced in ancient writings was peculiar to the literary class and was not shared by the population as a whole. This is proved by the importance attached to these devices in legislative texts, particularly those from Athens. They show that manual dexterity and skilled labor were in actual fact held in great regard.[158]

The question, however, is: held in high regard by whom? Workers, managers, and the military naturally respected machinery and manual skill. Nevertheless, the attitudes of the masses in antiquity are difficult to document and not relevant to the views of the tiny scientific elite. Scientists were intellectuals with private incomes or wealthy patrons. As such, they were "gentlemen" and shared the biases of the aristocracy, even in those rare cases when a scientist had risen from a lowly origin. To moderns, it seems contradictory that Greek scientists were patronizing toward labor and technology (some of which they invented), but it is anachronistic to deny the fact. The philosopher was the ideal, and theory was idolized, even by Aristotle who appreciated laboratory methods. Modern society, too, venerates the Einstein type of theorist over Edison and the industrious plodders. In Hellas, scientists preferred the head over the hand and considered theoretical ingenuity more valuable than grimy experiments. Even the great inventor Archimedes felt that mechanics was sordid while mathematics liberated the soul.[159] Perhaps later writers put these words into Archimedes' mouth, but it is more likely that the most renowned scientist of the third century shared the class biases of the Greek intelligentsia.

In the Hellenic world, a considerable gap existed between the theoretical and applied sciences. Aristotle complained of this situation:

We notice that the geometricians are quite unable to apply their scientific proofs in practice. When it comes to dividing a piece of land, or to any other operation on magnitudes and spaces, the surveyors can do it because of their experience, but those who are concerned with mathematics and with the reasons for these things, while they may know how it is to be done, cannot do it.[160]

The history of much Greek science is the record of men who, according to Aristotle, were divorced from the practical application of knowledge. As a corollary, Hellenic scientists often discarded empirical method when evidence clashed with a persuasive theory. Plato warned astronomers not to be misled by the apparent paths of celestial bodies, but rather to contemplate the circular perfection of the heavens with the eye of the soul.[161] Hamstrung by the dogma that celestial motion was perfect and circular, Greek astronomers expended great ingenuity to reconcile the erratic behavior of the planets with their presumed circular motion. In Hellas, most astronomical doctrines were based on intuition and supported by elaborate mathematical proofs. In the milieu of Greek science, sensory perception was subordinate to rationalism and secondary to mathematics.

A high esteem for intuitive reasoning made Greek scientists susceptible to the lure of elitism. From the image of the mathematical wizard Pythagoras grew the tradition of a scientific elite which cast a long shadow in the intellectual history of Europe. The myth of secret Pythagorean wisdom accompanied revivals of Platonism and persisted in Europe until the seventeenth century A.D. Both Copernicus and Kepler were convinced that they had recovered Pythagorean astronomical arcana. Only with the greatest reluctance did Copernicus reveal his "Pythagorean" views to general readers.[162] His scholarly reserve had Platonic precedents. According to Aristotle, Plato communicated his secret doctrines orally to only a select audience.[163] In the Seventh Epistle, Plato explained his reluctance to publish arcane truths:

I do not think that the examination . . . of these questions would be of any benefit to men, except to a few, i.e. to those who could with a little guidance discover the truth by themselves. Of the rest, some would be filled with an ill-founded and quite unbecoming disdain, and some with an exaggerated and foolish elation, as if they had learned something grand.[164] *

While Aristotle and his followers were not as reticent as Plato, many Greek scientists were imbued with the notion that higher truths were reserved for superior men.

In the Greek world, scholarly aloofness was often prompted by snobbery, but discretion was occasionally a contributing factor. Hellenic society did not always look with favor on ideas which scientists entertained. Although intellectuals fancied themselves members of an elite, the scientist stood alone when the wrath of society was aimed at him as an individual. For their citizens, many Greek cities provided more freedom and participation in government than any modern democracy, and most Athenians of Pericles' time would view the American system of representation with horror. Among the Greeks, free speech was not limited by libel laws or respect for truth. Yet, the liberties of a citizen were derived from society and were revocable by the community. In Greece, a citizen had no inalienable human rights; his liberties were dependent solely on the state. When faced with condemnation by society, a Greek had no legitimate appeal other than a plea for mercy; in practice, he took to flight. All of his freedoms were the result of a Greek's membership in a community; none were based on his status as a human being. Some poets and philosophers alluded to "unwritten laws" or religious obligations which were equally binding for pious men. Written

* From *Plato's Epistles*, translated by Glenn R. Morrow, copyright (c) 1962 by the Bobbs-Merrill Company, reprinted by permission of the publishers.

or not, the laws had precedence over individual rights in Hellas.

Although Pericles extolled Athens as the "school of Hellas," [165] most distinguished scientists and philosophers who graced the famous city were aliens. Attracted to the imperial city by prospects of wealth, visiting lecturers lacked the feeble protection of citizenship and were dependent upon individual patrons. In times of stress, Athenian hospitality was easily revocable. The famous blasphemy indictments of the fifth century were largely directed against the itinerant sages who had made Athens the intellectual capital of the Greek world.

The first resident scientist at Athens, Anaxagoras of Clazomenae, was also the first victim of Attic bigotry. The great scientist migrated to Athens, perhaps in the archonship of Calliades in 480, and remained in the city for thirty years.[166] Among his pupils was the future democratic chief Pericles, whose enlightened views on natural phenomena later became a political liability.[167] Nevertheless, Pericles profited from his scientific education and calmed his fellow citizens during the solar eclipse of 431, unlike Nicias who was dismayed by a lunar eclipse a few years later.[168] Although Anaxagoras had no interest in politics and insisted that he was a citizen of heaven,[169] the scientist was a former Persian subject in Athens at a time when relations were strained with Persia. About 450, Anaxagoras was indicted for impiety and for corresponding with Persian agents. While his espionage activities are unlikely, Anaxagoras' view that the sun was a large mass of burning metal was blasphemous by Greek standards. Despite Pericles' influence, the astronomer had to flee from Athens and was condemned to death in absentia.[170] In Asia Minor, the city of Lampsacus welcomed the refugee scientist and honored him with a monument after his death.[171] His most lasting gift to Lampsacus was an annual holiday for children which Anaxagoras had asked the city fathers to hold on the anniversary of his death.

At Athens the official lunar calendar was often inaccurate and frequently altered for political and festival purposes. About 433, the Athenian astronomer Meton advised the city to employ a nineteen-year cycle of intercalations that reconciled the solar and lunar years.[172] However, the Attic government preferred to retain its anarchic lunar calendar. Although the Metonic cycle

did not become the basis of the Athenian civil calendar,[173] the
city honored the astronomer with a statue for his services to
the community.[174] According to a late tradition, Meton was also
an astrologer and foresaw the disaster that awaited the Athenian
expedition to Sicily in 415. Since he had been asked to join the
enterprise, Meton burned down his house in order to stay in
Athens when the fleet sailed.[175] The astronomer was a well-
known public figure, and Aristophanes featured Meton in the
Birds as a pompous fraud who confused city planning with
squaring the circle. In the comedy, the leader of the birds,
Pisthetaerus, was bothered by various human pests including
Meton, who offered his services as a city planner:

METON.
 I would survey for you the Realm of Air . . .
 Partition it in lots.
PISTHETAERUS.
 For heaven's sake, who are you, anyway?
METON.
 Meton, by name. All Hellas knows me! . . .
PISTHETAERUS.
 Say, what have you there?
METON.
 Measures, to plot the sky.
 To illustrate, the air, in total form,
 Is very like an oven top. So, then,
 Applying from above this metric arc,
 With compasses thereon. . . . You follow?
PISTHETAERUS.
 No!
METON.
 I use a ruler, thus, until at length
 The circle has been squared, and in the midst
 A market place is set, from which the streets
 Are drawn, to radiate as from a star,
 The beams of which, itself a circle, shine
 Straight forth to every point.
PISTHETAERUS.
 The man's a Thales! Meton . . .
METON.
 What is it?

PISTHETAERUS.
  Well . . . you know I love you . . .
  Do me a favor—go away from here!
METON.
  Am I in danger?
PISTHETAERUS.
  As in Spartan law,
  Today is moving day for foreigners.
  The town is in a tumult.
METON.
  Civil war?
PISTHETAERUS.
  Oh, no.
METON.
  Then, what?
PISTHETAERUS.
  Unanimous consent to wallop every humbug in the land!
METON.
  I'll just slip off.
PISTHETAERUS.
  You'd better. . . . No, too late! They're after you.[176]

To the delight of the audience, the comic scientist was beaten
and driven off stage. Although the caricature of Meton was also
aimed against the famed city planner Hippodamus of Miletus,[177]
it is significant that Aristophanes' ridicule of the great astronomer
would provoke laughter from an Athenian audience.

The apparent discrepancy between Meton's previous honors
and the lampoon that Aristophanes delivered against him in
414 reflected the effect of the decree of Diopeithes against astronomy. In 431, Athens had become involved in a major war
with Sparta despite the warning of the Delphic oracle that
Apollo would support the Spartans. In 430, the city of Athens
was crowded with refugees who lived in squalor while the
Spartans ravaged the country districts of Attica. Within the
beleaguered city, plague broke out and many Athenians perished.
The plague may have been endemic typhus, glanders, or even
measles.[178] Perhaps it was a disease no longer known to modern
medicine, but the people of Athens viewed the plague as the
work of Apollo, the god of pestilence. Religious hysteria swept
the city, and the diviner Diopeithes persuaded the Assembly

to pass a decree banning atheists and prohibiting the teaching of astronomy.[179] Since he also concerned himself with security regulations for the port of Athens, Diopeithes was probably a McCarthyesque opportunist rather than a sincere bigot.[180] After the Sicilian debacle of 413, soothsayers were unpopular in Athens, and Diopeithes apparently was indicted under one of his own security decrees.[181] Expelled from Athens, the diviner offered his services to Sparta and became involved in a dispute over the succession to the Spartan throne.[182] Because Plutarch carelessly connected the decree of Diopeithes with the indictment of Anaxagoras, the British historian J. B. Bury inferred that "the study of astronomy was forbidden for nearly half a century (up to the archonship of Eucleides in 403 B.C.) in the city which was the centre of Greek culture." [183] However, any link between the persecution of Anaxagoras and the decree of Diopeithes raises serious chronological difficulties, and the public honors to Meton about 433 obviously preceded the ban on astronomy.

As far as is known, no astronomer was indicted under the decree of Diopeithes, which apparently intimidated the scientists who resided in Athens. However, two famous intellectuals, Protagoras and Diagoras, ran afoul of the law against atheism. The great sophist Protagoras of Abdera had drawn up laws for the city of Thurii [184] and was a personal friend of Pericles. Protagoras was also a relativist who believed that absolute knowledge of the existence of the gods was impossible.[185] Atheists were never popular in Greece, and Athens had suffered a naval defeat in 440 at the hands of Melissus of Samos who held an agnostic position on the existence of the gods.[186] Perhaps, Melissus' views were fresh in the minds of the voters when they passed the decree of Diopeithes in the early years of the Peloponnesian War. According to tradition, during one of his visits to Athens, the aged Protagoras was indicted for atheism and expelled from the city. The attack on the philosopher was credited to Pythodorus who was one of the oligarchic rulers of Athens in 411.[187] However, Plato claimed that Protagoras died at the age of seventy after forty years of uninterrupted success.[188] According to E. R. Dodds, "Plato is speaking of Protagoras' international reputation *as a teacher*, which would not be diminished by an Athenian heresy-hunt." [189] The action against

Protagoras could also have taken place shortly after the Peace of Nicias in 421 when the mood of Athens was pious and conservative.[190] Although a formal indictment of Protagoras is debatable, the Attic government collected his agnostic books and burned them in the market place.[191] During the stress of the Sicilian expedition, Athens prosecuted individuals who had allegedly revealed religious mysteries.[192] In the atmosphere of hysteria, the outspoken poet, Diagoras of Melos, was driven from the city on a charge of atheism.[193] Like Protagoras, Diagoras was famed for his sarcastic comments on conventional religion,[194] but neither man can be considered a martyr to science.

Plutarch, who worried over godless scientists, commented on the blasphemy indictments of fifth century Athens:

The first man to attempt to explain in writing the illumination and eclipse of the moon was Anaxagoras, and his account was the boldest and most lucid of all. But this was a recent theory, nor did it enjoy much repute; in fact, it was still treated as a secret, confined to a small circle and only communicated with great caution rather than with confidence. Public opinion was instinctively hostile toward natural philosophers and visionaries, as they were called, since it was generally believed that they belittled the power of the gods by explaining it away as nothing more than the operation of irrational causes and blind forces acting by necessity. For this reason even Protagoras was driven into exile and Anaxagoras imprisoned, till Pericles managed to rescue him with great difficulty, while Socrates, although he had nothing whatever to do with this kind of speculation, was nevertheless put to death for his connection with philosophy. It was not until later that the glorious fame of Plato shone forth and served not only through the example of his life but also through his teaching that the forces of nature are subject to a higher principle, to dispel the odium which had attached itself to such theories, thereby enabling them to circulate freely.[195]

Plutarch's anachronistic sermon was oversimplified in order to show Plato to good advantage. In reality, the decree of Diopeithes was nullified by the general revision of Athenian laws which took place when democracy was restored in 403. By the beginning of the fourth century, a book by Anaxagoras could be purchased in the Athenian market place for one drachma.[196]

Ironically, evidence for the ease with which Anaxagoras' books could be purchased comes from the defense plea of Socrates on trial for his life. Although the restored democracy usually acted with exemplary restraint, Socrates had mocked politicians for decades and in 399 his enemies took their revenge. The old philosopher was charged with impiety and corrupting the young. In the popular mind, Socrates was mistaken for a sophist who undermined religion by teaching science. Although Socrates easily proved that he was not a godless scientist, it is significant that the charge was made. In the *Clouds,* Aristophanes had portrayed Socrates as a subversive professor who mumbled blasphemies about the heavens while his students turned against their parents—the absurd image reappears in history whenever shallow minds seek a scapegoat in science. Commenting on a character in the *Clouds,* Victor Ehrenberg observes:

Of science most people knew nothing, and the complete blankness of Strepsiades' mind when he hears of astronomy and geometry reflects, though in comic exaggeration, the widespread ignorance of what was supposed to be an important part of the teaching of some of the sophists.[197]

Socrates had actually rejected science years before when he attended a lecture by Anaxagoras and the astronomer had made no mention of ethics.[198] According to Xenophon, Socrates warned his friends not to pry into the secrets of nature lest they go mad like Anaxagoras.[199] Because of his arrogant behavior in court and his former friendship with the predatory politicians Critias and Alcibiades, Socrates was found guilty of corrupting the young and was sentenced to death. His persecutors expected Socrates to flee as Anaxagoras and Protagoras had done, but the old philosopher resolved to die for his beliefs and shame the scientist and the sophist who had scrambled to safety.

The fate of Socrates was a unique tragedy in a troubled time, and Athens ceased molesting troublesome intellectuals. The great atomist Democritus of Abdera complained: "I came to Athens and no one there knew me." [200] Under the direction of Aristotle, science flourished among the Peripatetics at the Lyceum, but many scholars preferred the curriculum of mathematics and Platonism at the Academy. In the brief anti-Macedonian outburst of 323, Aristotle was driven from the city as the supposed friend of the late Alexander. Dying in exile in Chalcis, Aristotle wearily confessed: "The more solitary and isolated I am, the more I have come to study myths." [201] While Athens returned to the Macedonian yoke, Theophrastus of Eresus supervised the study of science at the Lyceum. In 317, the city was occupied by the Macedonian king Cassander. Because his father Antipater had favored Aristotle, Cassander set up the Peripatetic Demetrius of Phalerum as governor of Athens. For ten years, Demetrius ruled the city with erratic indulgence. When the irreverent Theodorus of Cyrene shocked public opinion with atheistic jokes, Demetrius rescued Theodorus from a blasphemy indictment and hurried him out of the city.[202] The Lyceum prospered and a Peripatetic inventor provided Demetrius with a mechanical snail which moved through the streets and spat out saliva.[203] Like most intellectuals in power, Demetrius made a few ineffectual attempts to impose his moralistic views on society.

When the warlord Demetrius Poliorcetes captured Athens in 307, Demetrius of Phalerum fled to Alexandria and the Athenians took revenge on the Peripatetics. The Assembly passed the ill-conceived decree of Sophocles which drove Theophrastus into exile and prescribed the death penalty for any philosopher who taught without official approval.[204] However, the Assembly soon reconsidered and punished Sophocles for having proposed the ban on scientific freedom.[205] Theophrastus returned to Athens where Peripatetic research continued until the center of advanced studies shifted to Alexandria in the early third century. Although Athenian democrats could take little pride in the decrees of Diopeithes and Sophocles, the only scientist to suffer at Athens had been the astronomer Anaxagoras whose indictment had been primarily an expression of anti-Persian sentiment. Athens' reputation as the "school of Hellas" was tarnished by the occasional harassment of agnostics and atheists, but the city did not pursue a constant policy of persecuting scientists. The Athenian attitude toward science was not one of suppression but of indifference which fostered a sneering contempt for "woolly-headed professors."

TWO

The Hellenistic World

SCIENCE AND SUBSIDY

The Hellenistic age was dominated by the ghosts of Alexander and Aristotle. The kings who divided Alexander's empire demanded divine honors from their subjects and squandered their energies and treasures on endless dynastic wars. The Hellenistic era was an age of anxiety and Aristotle's rationalism had little appeal, for the Peripatetic philosophy could not provide peace of mind in a raging world. But, the scientific approach of Aristotle was preserved in the great research center at Alexandria and at courts where scholars enjoyed the bounty of royal patrons. According to an apocryphal Platonic epistle, "it is a law of nature that wisdom and great power go together; they exert a mutual attraction and are forever seeking to be united." [1] In the past, Olympic athletes had brought glory to the Greek city states, but Hellenistic kings subsidized science and gigantic constructions to awe the world.

According to the Peripatetic Theophrastus, scholars were true citizens of the world who could survive changes of fortune and find employment in any land. [2] His own life proves the claim, for Theophrastus enjoyed the patronage of King Cassander of Macedon and Ptolemy I of Egypt. [3] Although briefly expelled from Athens in 307, Theophrastus presided over the Lyceum for thirty-seven years and left the Peripatetic institute in a sound financial condition. [4] His pupil Strato earned enormous fees as the tutor of Ptolemy II and succeeded Theophrastus as head of the Lyceum in 286. [5] A distinguished student of pneumatics, Strato brought Aristotelian science to its logical conclusion when he abandoned the study of ethics in order to concentrate on scientific research.[6] To a degree, Strato's choice reflected the specialization that characterized the intelligentsia of the Hellenistic age. As knowledge and libraries expanded in the various disciplines, intellectuals were unable to cope with the enormous mass of specialized learning. In effect, scientists became more learned in their own fields and more ignorant of the total knowledge of the era.

By historical accident, many Greeks were scholars who otherwise would have been politicians. According to Polybius, Hellenic leaders turned to intellectual pursuits because the Macedonians and Romans deprived them of political activity.[7] Polybius' career confirms his thesis, for he had been a politician and became a historian under Roman rule. The conquest of Greece left intellectuals few avenues for advancement other than in the employ of kings. Whether wrapped in the mantle of a Stoic sage or engaged in research at Alexandria, the Hellenistic intellectual was in effect a courtier. Alexander had set the pattern for Hellenistic kings when he added Anaxarchus of Abdera to his entourage. On his campaigns in Persia, the king took time to discuss atomism and the infinity of worlds with Anaxarchus, who had studied under Democritus.[8] Under the pressure of court intrigue, Anaxarchus submerged his scientific interests and concentrated on winning the favor of Alexander.[9] When an Indian holy man shamed him for dancing attendance on a king, the scientist abandoned court life.[10] Later, Anaxarchus defied a petty tyrant on Cyprus and was tortured to death.[11] Few Greek scientists would emulate Anaxarchus' change of heart.

Most Hellenistic intellectuals actively sought the patronage of kings. A notable exception was the philosopher Stilpo of Megara who went into hiding when Ptolemy I wanted to carry him off to Egypt.[12] In 307, the Peripatetic Demetrius of Phalerum fled from Athens to Alexandria, where he soon became involved in the power struggles of the Ptolemaic court.[13] According to tradition, the famed Peripatetic helped to organize the Museum, the institute for advanced studies in Alexandria. Demetrius' friend, Theodorus of Cyrene, who had been driven from Athens for his irreligious views, served Ptolemy I as an envoy to King Lysimachus.[14] Because of his impudent wit, the famous atheist oc-

casionally angered his royal hosts, but it is doubtful that
Theodorus was executed for impiety as a late source claimed.[15]
Few philosophers feared their patrons. Asked what he had
gained from philosophy, one sage, Ctesibius of Chalcis, candidly
replied, "Free dinners." [16] His patron Antigonus Gonatas also
employed the convivial Stoic Persaeus as governor of Corinth.[17]
Another worldly Stoic, Sphaerus, composed propaganda tracts
for Cleomenes III of Sparta and received patronage from Ptolemy
III and Ptolemy IV.[18] The philosopher Euphantus of Olynthus
dedicated a popular work on monarchy to his royal friend and
former pupil, Antigonus Doson of Macedon.[19] As head of the
Academy, Arcesilaus shunned the aid of Antigonus Gonatas but
accepted the bounty of King Eumenes of Pergamum who was
also a patron of the Peripatetic Lyco.[20] With Roman domination
of the East, the Greek intelligentsia changed employers and
sought the favor of Roman generals. The Stoic Panaetius was a
close friend of Scipio Aemilianus, the destroyer of Carthage, and
Caesar's rival Pompey supported the Stoic Posidonius who was
an encyclopedic writer on natural history.[21] In their roles as courtiers, Greek scholars learned the arts of discretion and subser-
vience.

Early in the Hellenistic age, the generals of Alexander seized
crowns and assumed divine status. Even the democrats of Athens
groveled before the self-made gods and prayed to Demetrius
Poliorcetes: "The other gods do not exist or are far away; either
they do not hear or do not care. But we see you here, not in
wood or stone, but truly!" [22] The cults of the divine kings served
the same purpose as does worship of the state in modern times.
At Cassander's court, the scholar Euhemerus buttressed the concept of divine monarchy. According to Euhemerus, the traditional gods were actually great men of the past who had been
deified because they were just rulers or inventors of the arts and
sciences.[23] Other Hellenistic writers followed Euhemerus' suggestion and projected royal patronage of science back into the
remote world of myth: "At the court of Osiris and Isis, special
honors were bestowed on men who discovered the arts or invented useful devices." [24] The historian Diodorus even insisted
that the Homeric king Agamemnon had exempted physicians
from military service and other obligatory duties to the state.[25]

However, obligations to the state, which the Greeks called liturgies, were characteristic of the Hellenistic age and not the Homeric era.

At court, Hellenistic scientists were rewarded with wealth and generally exempted from liturgies. The architect Deinocrates was so anxious to attract the attention of Alexander that he appeared before the king dressed as Hercules. When the surprised Alexander asked the significance of his costume, Deinocrates replied that he could shape Mount Athos into an image of the king.[26] Alexander assigned Deinocrates to more practical tasks, and the architect displayed his talents in planning the metropolis of Alexandria in Egypt.[27] In the third century, the famous engineer Archimedes visited Ptolemaic Egypt and gave his hosts a design for a water screw which was soon used to raise canal water over levees into irrigated fields.[28] In Spain, his invention was employed in pumping water from flooded mines.[29] A relative of King Hiero II of Syracuse, Archimedes served the Sicilian city as a master mechanic and designer of stupendous weapons.[30] Archimedes' trip to Alexandria was a pilgrimage to the scientific capital of the age.

Greek science had its golden age during the third century in Ptolemaic Egypt. Only a wealthy society could support such an expensive research center as the Alexandrian Museum, which was the intellectual ornament of the Ptolemaic state. The Ptolemies squeezed taxes from their subjects by combining the bureaucratic thoroughness of the Pharaohs with the money-grubbing ingenuity of Greek businessmen.[31] Except for slaves who were condemned to the mines, there was little slavery in Ptolemaic Egypt, for "native labor was too cheap and too thoroughly controlled for slavery to be worthwhile."[32] In a sense, all subjects of the Ptolemies were slaves because the government regulated the activities of all classes with amazing thoroughness. In a characteristic memorandum, an Egyptian official ordered his subordinates to take care that no graft would occur:

Every resident of the country must clearly understand and believe that all acts of this kind have been stopped, and that they are freed from the bad conditions of the past, for now no one has a right to do what he likes, but everything is managed in the best possible way. Thus, you will make the countryside secure and increase the revenue considerably.[33]

Under the Ptolemies, men were controlled as never before in the long history of despotism.

The source of Ptolemaic wealth did not disturb the specialists at the Museum, who enjoyed the bounty of the kings.[34] The poet Theocritus hailed Ptolemy as "the best paymaster a free man can have." [35] For two centuries, scientists flocked to Egypt, and some were giants of astronomy, mathematics, or medicine— Euclid, Aristarchus, Eratosthenes, Herophilus, and Erasistratus. The poet Timon of Phlius growled:

> In the thronging land of Egypt,
> There are many that are feeding,
> Many scribblers on papyrus,
> Ever ceaselessly contending,
> In the bird-coop of the Muses.[36]

The Ptolemies considered the Museum a monument to their splendor and expected that some scholars would invent useful devices. Later, the geographer Strabo saw the Museum under Roman jurisdiction:

The Museum is part of the royal palaces. It has a covered walk with seats and a large building which contains the messhall of the men of learning who live at the Museum and hold property in common. A priest is in charge of the Museum; he was formerly appointed by the kings but now is chosen by Caesar.[37]

Under Ptolemaic rule, the members of the Museum were exempt from taxes [38] and enjoyed a sanctuary of privilege in a land of exploitation.

At the Museum, scholars and scientists had leisure to pursue their studies, access to the finest libraries, and the opportunity to discuss matters with other resident specialists. In view of the crudity of ancient tools and the lack of well-equipped laboratories, the Museum cannot be compared in quality or quantity with modern scientific research centers.[39] However, by the standards of antiquity, the Museum was a remarkable innovation and a milestone in the history of science and patronage. The example of Egypt prompted rival monarchs to similarly endow scientists and learning. Antioch boasted an excellent library, and the Seleucids employed the great physician Erasistratus before he moved to Alexandria.[40] At Pergamum, the Attalids supported a major medical school and a library second only to the collections in Egypt. Hellenistic society appreciated literature, and the kings encouraged research in the humanities as well as science.

Alexandria was a cosmopolitan center, and the citizens boasted that it was the first "world city." In its heyday, the great Alexandrian Library was headed by men of the caliber of Eratosthenes, whose method for calculating the circumference of the earth was a masterpiece of geometric imagination. Eratosthenes reflected the cosmopolitanism of Alexandria in his comment on Aristotle's conviction that Greeks were friends and "barbarians" were enemies. According to Eratosthenes, Aristotle should have distinguished between the good and bad in each ethnic group as did Alexander.[41] In an age that respected cleverness and delighted in gadgets, vertical social mobility was possible even for a barber's son. The Alexandrian Ctesibius first attracted attention by hanging a mirror on hidden weights in his barber shop. The inventor soon enjoyed the patronage of Ptolemy II and Ptolemy III and constructed water clocks and automata which were moved by pneumatic and hydraulic pressures. In the temple of Arsinoë, one of Ctesibius' devices played music as wine was poured through it.[42] At the Museum, the study of pneumatic principles continued for centuries, and Hero of Alexandria experimented with steam turbines in 62 A.D. Hero also described a temple vending machine that dispensed holy water when a five-drachma coin was dropped into a slot.[43] It is noteworthy that the ingenuity of Ctesibius and Hero was applied to contriving gadgets for the state and religious establishments.

Physicians were expected to serve the Ptolemaic state with more than pure research. The medical staff of the Museum supervised sanitation in Egypt and provided care for members of the military.[44] According to the Roman medical writer Celsus, the Egyptian government furnished the physicians Herophilus and Erasistratus with condemned criminals for vivisection.[45] The two great scientists were interested in the function of the motor nervous system which could be observed by damaging parts of the brain or severing crucial nerves. Although some modern historians feel that the practice of human vivisection in Alexandria was a canard, Celsus believed the charge and condemned the inhumanity of Hellenistic doctors.[46] Comparable abuses in modern times add weight to the probability of cruel practices in Alexandrian medicine.

The Museum and the Library reflected the grandiose taste of the early Ptolemies, who were obsessed with gigantism. On the island of Pharos, a great lighthouse, more than 400 feet high, towered over the harbor of Alexandria.[47] The engineer Sostratus of Cnidus built the lighthouse for Ptolemy II and served the same monarch as a diplomat. According to the late writer Athenaeus:

[Ptolemy II] surpassed many kings in wealth and in ships. His two largest vessels had thirty banks of oars; another had twenty, and four had thirteen. . . . He had more than 4,000 ships sailing [the sea]. As for the number of books, the establishment of libraries, and the collections at the Museum, why speak, since all men know of them! [48]

His grandson Ptolemy IV possessed a ship which was 420 feet long and had forty banks of oars; he also owned a yacht 300 feet long. Both ships were elaborately equipped and served as floating palaces.[49] The Sicilian ruler Hiero II constructed a mammoth boat, the "Lady of Syracuse," which rivaled the Egyptian vessels in ostentatious luxury. Hiero's ship was armed with catapults which could fire 180-pound stones and hurl 18-foot missiles within a range of 600 feet. Since no harbor in Sicily could accommodate the giant boat, Hiero renamed the vessel the "Lady of Alexandria" and gave it to his fellow yacht fancier, Ptolemy IV.[50] Such gargantuan ships served no commercial or military purpose and were only constructed to display the resources of Hellenistic states.

To the peoples of antiquity, exploration beyond the limits of the known world was as fascinating as the lure of outer space is to moderns. To satisfy his curiosity and fill the Alexandrian zoo, Ptolemy II sent expeditions deep into Africa for elephants, odd beasts, and a giant serpent which was brought back with great difficulty.[51] His collection also included a polar bear "whose journey south must have been exciting." [52] Perhaps with an eye to Indian Ocean trade, Ptolemy III sent explorers to the Somali coast and the shores of Arabia.[53] Since the seventh century B.C., the circumnavigation of Africa had been feasible. On the orders of the Saite Pharaoh Necho, a Phoenician fleet had sailed around Africa from East to West.[54] In the fifth century, a Persian magus appeared in Sicily and claimed to have made the ocean voyage around Africa.[55] According to the Stoic Posidonius, the trip was again attempted in the second century by the ship captain Eudoxus of Cyzicus. During the reign of Ptolemy VII, an Indian vessel was washed ashore in Egypt and the sole survivor of the crew offered to guide a party back to India. Eudoxus made the voyage and returned with a ship full of perfumes and gems, but Ptolemy confiscated Eudoxus' share of the cargo. When Cleopatra III sent Eudoxus back to India, the adventuresome seaman was shipwrecked below Ethiopia on his return trip. There he found a ship's prow which had come from the Southwest. Back in Alexandria, some sailors identified the horse-shaped prow as part of a ship that had never returned to Cadiz. Excited by the implications of his discovery, Eudoxus assembled an expedition in Spain and sailed down the West coast of Africa. After various mishaps, the intrepid explorer outfitted another ship in Spain and sailed into the unknown.[56] While the story of a prow from Cadiz invites suspicion, the earlier voyage to India is probable and suggests an awareness of the pattern of the monsoon winds across the Indian Ocean.[57] According to Strabo, "all men who have voyaged along the shores of Africa, whether they started from the Red Sea or from the Pillars of Hercules, have always turned back . . . because of the great difficulties of the trip." [58] However, Strabo's statement was too sweeping, for he discounted Necho's expedition. The voyage around Africa from the West had always been possible but it probably was not realized until the time of Vasco da Gama.[59]

While few men in antiquity rounded the Cape of Good Hope, greater success was achieved with the passage to India.[60] In Ptolemaic times, trade with India was extensive and expanded under Roman rule with 120 ships a year sailing from Egypt to India.[61] Through contact with Hellenistic traders and diplomats, some Indians became interested in the West. When the Maurya ruler Bindusara asked Antiochus I to sell him a Greek philosopher, the Seleucid king replied that the commodity was not for sale.[62] Bindusara's pious son Asoka hoped to convert the Hellenistic peoples and dispatched Buddhist missionaries to Antiochus II, Ptolemy II, Antigonus Gonatas, Magas of Cyrene, and Alexander of Epirus.[63] Unfortunately, the fate of Asoka's missionaries is unknown. If the Buddhists reached the West, their gospel did not impress the kings who were respectively an alcoholic, a bureaucrat, a troubled dynast, a mountain of fat, and a military adventurer. At best, the missionaries would have been considered fakirs and their sermons no more successful than Saint Paul's speech at Athens.[64] During the reign of Augustus, the Peripatetic Nicolaus of Damascus met three Indian envoys at Antioch who were on their way to Rome to present gifts to the ruler of the world.* In their party was a sage who later immolated himself at Athens.[65] Although the Far East was still remote, the conquests of Alexander had opened much of Asia to the Greeks [66] and ideas flowed freely across national borders.

In the Hellenistic age, libraries expanded and book dealers did a thriving trade. The Attalid kings of Pergamum maintained a splendid library,[67] but the greatest collection of books was assembled by the Ptolemies at Alexandria. Ancient writers were careless with numbers and exaggerated the size of the Alexandrian Library. Supposedly, Demetrius of Phalerum began the collection with 200,000 volumes and hoped to reach a half million.[68] Later, Caesar's troops accidentally burned 40,000 books, but Antony soon gave Cleopatra 200,000 volumes which he had extorted from Pergamum.[69] As statistics, such figures are worthless, but the holdings of the Library were very large. Although a number of books stored near the waterfront suffered damage when Caesar's men set fire to the Egyptian fleet, the loss did not hamper Strabo, Athenaeus, and other scholars who used the

---

* A garbled account of the three Indian travelers may lie behind the tradition of the Three Magi in the Jesus story.

Alexandrian Library. Probably more books at Alexandria were lost through wear and carelessness than in riots and wars.

Books were often coveted by rulers and collectors. During the conquest of Macedon in 168, the Roman general Aemilius Paullus seized the royal library as his personal booty.[70] In the third century, Aristotle's manuscripts and the personal library of Theophrastus had passed into the hands of the bibliophile Neleus of Scepias. His heirs hid the collection in a trench to save it from being confiscated by Eumenes II of Pergamum. The scrolls were damaged by moisture and insects and had to be recopied when Apellicon of Teos bought the collection.* However, Apellicon's copyists made many errors in restoring the texts, which no longer agreed with the copies of Aristotle's books in the Alexandrian Library. In the first century B.C., the dictator Sulla carried off Apellicon's collection to Rome where book dealers made more copies with even more errors. According to Strabo, the booksellers "are poor copyists and did not collate the texts. This always happens when books are copied for sale, both here and at Alexandria." [71] Since books were often badly copied and private collections were sometimes lost, scholars welcomed the great state libraries at Alexandria, Pergamum, and Rome.

Like books, intellectuals sometimes received rough handling in the Hellenistic age. The price for patronage often came high, for the prominent physician Chrysippus was manhandled and beaten at the Ptolemaic court.[72] When the philosopher Hegesias preached on the merits of suicide, Ptolemy II stopped his lectures as detrimental to the public good.[73] The same ruler crucified the Homeric critic Zoilus for some obscure affront.[74] In Alexandria, the social sciences did not receive state support, and apparently democrats and Cynics were not welcome at the Museum. Dissent was unwise and scientists held aloof from social problems. An interest in politics was dangerous for subsidized scholars. After a long struggle for power with Ptolemy VI, Ptolemy VII emerged triumphant in 145 and took revenge on

---

* Possibly, the story of the misadventures of Aristotle's manuscripts was invented to add authority to the definitive edition of the Aristotelean corpus which was made by Andronicus of Rhodes about 70 B.C.

partisans of his brother. The Museum was purged of all members who had not demonstrated their loyalty to the cause of Ptolemy VII. The late writer Athenaeus gave an exaggerated account of the episode:

The Alexandrians were the teachers of all Greeks and barbarians at a time when education had collapsed because of the endless disorders which occurred under Alexander's successors. In the reign of the seventh Ptolemy, another renaissance of culture took place . . . when the king sent many Alexandrians into exile, filling the islands and cities with men who had been close to his brother—philologists, philosophers, mathematicians, musicians, painters, athletic trainers, physicians, and other professional men. Reduced to poverty, the refugees [earned a living] teaching their skills to other men.[75]

While the world beyond Alexandria was not as ignorant as Athenaeus claimed, the purge of the Museum demonstrated the precarious status of the scientists who staffed the greatest institute for advanced research in antiquity.

As the balance of political power shifted to the West, Egypt slid into decline and the Museum slowly changed:

After the time of Ptolemy VII . . . the vast wealth of Ptolemaic Egypt was largely used to bribe Rome. So, materially, the Museum-Library suffered. As the liberal sums spent on culture dwindled, it was impossible to maintain the amazing intellectual importance of these institutions. . . . The dons were drawn into the political vortex, and those not so inclined were silent. . . . The members taught more and sent their pupils throughout the world. They devoted less time to research, and the institution changed from a college of research into a university of learning. This change was completed under the emperors.[76]

The new role of the Museum was evident when a wing was added in honor of the Roman emperor Claudius. Since Claudius was an amateur historian, the faculty of the Museum adopted his histories of Carthage and Etruria for classroom use.[77] Under Roman patronage, the honors and tax-exemptions of Museum membership were extended to politicians and even athletes.[78] In the third century A.D., Athenaeus considered the professors at the Museum intellectual parasites, and the historian Philostratus described the institute as "a dining table in Egypt to which the most distinguished men in the world are invited." [79] Whether the educators were parasites or merely bookworms, the Museum under Roman rule was only a shadow of its former self.

WAR AND THE QUEST FOR CERTAINTY

The Hellenistic era was an age of spiritual anguish and a time of endless warfare. The planning of war is exciting not only for generals but also for politicians and scientists. In the quasi-peace of a cold war, the designing of weapons can be a consuming passion for specialists who are engaged in armament research. To a degree, the ultimate application of weapons may be ignored by designers and specialists who are entranced by the game of forcing nature to serve human ends. The general practice of divorcing scientists from the actual waging of war neatly solves the ethical problem of responsibility. However, the psychological bond between technicians and their tools is another matter, and many different emotions are involved in the design and use of weapons which can engulf cities in fire. As the artist finds release in clay and stone, the military scientist often projects himself in steel and fire. In antiquity too, scientists were hired to design and improve military machines, but few records survive of their views on the role of science in warfare. The literary evidence is often obscured by the customary Greek rationalization lauding pure research over crass application.

Despite the legendary ten-year siege of Troy, early Greek wars were brief and often decided by a single pitched battle. Although the Assyrians had developed siegecraft to a high art, the Hellenes were slow in devising machinery and methods for storming walled towns. In 440, Pericles used the simple machines of Artemon of Clazomenae against the walls of Samos, but the city held out for eight months.[80] During the Peloponnesian War, Athens was safe for a generation behind its great fortifications. In the fourth century, Greek warfare was revolutionized by Philip of Macedon and Dionysius I of Syracuse who employed specialists, engineers, and elaborate siege equipment. Later, the citizens of Tyre used ingenious defensive machines when the troops of Alexander attacked the city walls. One of the Tyrian devices deflected missiles in flight and lessened the effect of the Macedonian artillery. When Alexander's chief engineer Diades utilized borers, movable towers, and climbing machines,[81] the city was taken. As siegecraft improved, fortifications became more formidable and states were obliged to expend vast sums on military technology. The rich and powerful commercial cities of Marseilles and Rhodes spared no expense in procuring the finest armaments, arsenals, and technical experts.[82]

When the warlord Demetrius Poliorcetes laid siege to Rhodes in 304, the engineering and technical skills of Hellenistic scientists were displayed on a grand scale. The citizens of Rhodes crowded the parapets to gape with astonishment at the great machines that the invaders assembled before the walls.[83] With towers, rams, and catapults, Demetrius assaulted the city, but his attacks failed. As the siege dragged on, Rhodes was supplied with food by blockade runners from Egypt and Asia Minor.[84] Since the Rhodians were dissatisfied with their military engineer Diognetus, a visiting expert Callias of Aradus offered to build a crane that would destroy the moving towers of the enemy. When the city fathers replaced Diognetus with Callias, Demetrius hired the Athenian engineer Epimachus who constructed a mobile armored tower or *Helepolis* which was 150 feet high and could withstand the impact of a 360 pound missile. Callias was unable to build a counter-machine, and the Rhodians asked Diognetus to forgive their ingratitude and save the beleaguered state.[85] In an earlier campaign on Cyprus, Demetrius had lost a *Helepolis* when the enemy set fire to the tower.[86] But at Rhodes, the wily dynast took greater care and protected the *Helepolis* from night attacks and fire missiles.[87] Realizing that technology had reached its limits, Diognetus employed a cunning stratagem and flooded the ground around the *Helepolis* which bogged down in the mud and could not be moved.[88] Discouraged by the heroic resistance of the Rhodians and the failure of his weapons, Demetrius lifted the siege and sailed away.[89] The abandoned war machines were sold by the jubilant citizens of Rhodes who used the proceeds to build a colossal statue of Apollo which towered 120 feet over the harbor.[90] Both the *Helepolis* of Demetrius Poliorcetes and the

Colossus of Rhodes were symptomatic of Hellenistic obsession with size.

On a less spectacular level, scientific knowledge aided other cities under siege. Earlier, the generals of Darius the Great besieged the city of Barca in Libya and dug tunnels under its walls. The defenders located the tunnels by setting up bronze shields which would rattle when the Persians were digging underground.[91] In 214, a similar technique saved the city of Apollonia which was under siege by Philip V of Macedon. Aware that the Macedonians were digging tunnels under the walls, the city's military technician Trypho of Alexandria dug counter-tunnels where he hung bronze vessels which vibrated at the sound of digging. When the enemy sappers had been located, Trypho's men poured burning pitch and boiling oil into the Macedonian tunnels.[92] A few years later, the defenders of Ambracia used sheets of bronze to locate Roman sappers and cleared the Roman tunnel by blowing in pungent smoke with a blacksmith's bellows.[93] With a little knowledge of physics, the citizens of Barca, Apollonia, and Ambracia had located unseen enemies.

As Greek warfare became more complex and dependent on technology,[94] a need arose for technical military literature. In the fourth century, the experienced mercenary Aeneas Tacticus composed a military manual which dealt primarily with ruses in warfare and the suppression of internal subversion.[95] Pyrrhus of Epirus had the manual condensed for troop instruction, and Greek and Roman armies often followed Aeneas' recommendation to smear the tips of arrows with the venom of vipers, asps, and salamanders.[96] Many Hellenistic military tracts were skillful studies of the application of science and technology in warfare. The Russian historian Michael Rostovtzeff commented on the military literature of the Hellenistic age:

Distinguished scholars, acquainted with the achievements of pure science, applied themselves to this department of military technique and sometimes made spectacular discoveries. It will be sufficient to recall such well-known names as Ctesibius, Philon, Biton, and perhaps Heron and Athenaeus, and the most eminent and famous of them all,

Archimedes. Except Archimedes, all these scientists recorded their
inventions in special treatises . . . , and we are justified in supposing
that these books were extensively used by the technical staffs of the
Hellenistic armies and navies.[97]

The Hellenistic era also produced theorists on warfare. At the
court of Antiochus III, the Peripatetic Phormio lectured Hannibal on the art of war. With understandable impatience, the
great Carthaginian responded that Phormio was the most pitiful
of all the lunatics whom he had met.[98]

In the Hellenistic age, the state heavily subsidized military
research. Commenting on the construction of long-range catapults, the engineer Philo of Byzantium emphasized the importance of state aid in developing weapons:

Some of the ancients discovered that the diameter of the bore was
the basic element, principle, and measurement in the construction of
artillery. But it was necessary to determine this diameter not accidentally or haphazardly but by some definite method, by which one
could also determine the proportionate measurement for all magnitudes on the instrument. . . . The ancients did not succeed in deter-
mining this magnitude by test, because their trials were not conducted
on the basis of many different types of performance, but merely in
connection with the required performance. But the engineers who
came later, noting the errors of their predecessors and the results
of subsequent experiments, reduced the principle of construction to
a single basic element—the diameter of the circle that receives the
twisted skeins. Success in this work was recently achieved by the
Alexandrian engineers, who were heavily subsidized by kings eager
for fame and interested in the arts.[99]

This passage also confirms the employment of experimental
methods in antiquity. According to Philo, Ctesibius tried to
increase the force and range of catapults with compressed air,
and Dionysius of Alexandria devised a machine gun for firing
arrows.[100] However, ancient manufacturers did not achieve pre-
cision or resistance to stress in machinery, and the ingenious
weapons of Ctesibius and Dionysius were never employed on
the battlefield.

In 213, the acme of ancient scientific warfare was reached

during the Roman assault on Syracuse when the city was "defended by an old man with ropes and pulleys." For years, Archimedes had fortified Syracuse with elaborate weapons, and despite his age the great scientist directed the defense of the city against the Roman attack. When the Roman war machines approached the walls, Archimedes swept them away with cranes. With similar devices, he capsized Roman ships in the harbor and sank others by dropping heavy weights from a great height. The city walls were covered with catapults and cross-bows which were permanently set in place to mow down advancing infantry at specific ranges. The Roman soldiers soon became demoralized, and "when they saw a rope or beam projecting over the wall, they turned and ran screaming that Archimedes was aiming some machine at them." [101] One man's ingenuity kept the Roman army at bay, and legends later credited Archimedes with the unlikely feat of using mirrors to burn enemy ships with the rays of the sun.[102] By 211, the overconfident Syracusans had relaxed their vigilance and a treacherous mercenary admitted Roman troops into the city—two contingencies that the great scientist had not anticipated. The Roman commander sent officers to seize the inventor of the wonderful weapons. Before they could locate Archimedes, a common soldier had surprised the scientist in his study and had slain the old man.[103] In legends, the master mechanic lived on, and Leonardo da Vinci read in a novel that Archimedes served at the court of a Spanish king and constructed machines that sprayed burning pitch upon English ships.[104]

The achievements of Hellenistic technicians gave rise to fabulous tales of tactics and weapons. The British historian Sir Frank Adcock comments on such stories:

If I had a more robust faith than I possess in the veracity of tradition, I could adduce the Messenians' story of their native hero Aristomenes that he floated down from a high cliff by using his shield as a parachute. I would not think it proper to limit the acts of faith, and I would commend to consideration the account in Cornelius Nepos and Justin of how Hannibal, when in command of a Hellenistic fleet, sent his sailors on shore to collect poisonous snakes alive. These he enclosed in fragile jars and propelled them into the enemy ships to spread abroad alarm and despondency, to match, I suppose, the uneasiness of mind of his own gallant marines as they enlisted these ambiguous allies. The instinctive, perhaps pedestrian, reluctance that I feel to give whole-hearted credence to this story does not remove my high regard for the unknown tactician who invented it and fathered it on Hannibal. And I have no serious doubt that this inventor was a Greek.[105]

While neither tale warrants belief, the range of military imagination did not always exceed the limits of practicality, for the Arabs of Hatra filled clay pots with poisonous insects and hurled them into the ranks of their enemies.[106] Despite the accomplishments of Hellenistic engineers and specialists, Greek warfare never attained the manic perfection of modern war. Although the ancients butchered as much as they could, their weapons were inadequate for mass destruction. The decisive factors in ancient warfare were the common sense of generals and the fighting spirit of their men.

In the Hellenistic age, not everyone was entranced with the ingenuity of scientists who served the military. The Cynic Onesicritus praised a Utopian people in India who cultivated "only one science, medicine, for evil is produced by the other sciences, especially that of war." [107] Generally, the Cynics were hostile to science and regarded scientists as frauds. When he heard an astronomer lecturing on the eccentric orbits of the planets, Diogenes interrupted the speaker and pointed to the audience: "Don't lie! The real eccentrics are not up there but down here!" [108] The Cynics were puritanical anarchists and only voiced the protest of a noisy minority. On the other hand, the Stoics used science to demonstrate that Providence controlled human affairs through astral influences. Relying on astrology, the Stoics defended the status quo as divinely ordained and were invariably conservative in politics.[109] When Antigonus Gonatas considered restoring democracy in Eretria, Stoic advisers dissuaded the king.[110] Centuries later, Stoics were active against the democrats at Tarsus.[111] Of the major Hellenistic philosophies, Stoicism was most popular among intellectuals who were committed to the established order.

Only by contrast with the Stoics could the Epicureans be considered liberal. Although women and possibly Negroes were admitted to the circle of Epicurus,[112] the philosopher did not intend to upset the social order and strongly disapproved of any involvement in politics.[113] Commenting on the Epicurean Aristion who led the Athenian rebellion against Rome in 88 B.C.,[114] the historian Appian expressed surprise over the political activity of an Epicurean.[115] Serenity was the aim of Epicurus who considered conventional religion and fear of the afterlife to be unnecessary mental disturbances. A noted Marxist historian of science, Benjamin Farrington, has argued that Epicurus' attacks on popular religion constituted a threat to state cults, particularly at Rome.[116] However, the ancient evidence does not support Farrington's thesis that Epicureanism was a militant atheistic creed. In 173 B.C., two Epicureans were banished from Rome for advocating hedonism.[117] But Epicurean attacks on religion did not prompt reprisals by the state, for only evangelists and miracle-mongers were offended.[118] Cicero teased Caesar's assassin Cassius for associating with Epicureans,[119] and most Romans criticized the school of Epicurus only because it was apolitical.[120]

Because Epicurus endorsed the atomic theory of Democritus, Marxists have hailed him as a fearless champion of science. However, Epicurus was an explicit pragmatist with regard to scientific truth:

Remember that, like everything else, knowledge of celestial phenomena, whether taken along with other things or in isolation, has no other end in view than peace of mind and firm conviction. We do not seek to wrest by force what is impossible, nor to understand all matters equally well. . . . Our one need is untroubled existence.[121]

Such an attitude would be anathema to a scientific positivist.

Instead of endangering established cults, science often helped religion in the Greek world. Everywhere, men with mechanical skills constructed temple miracles to stimulate piety. In the temples of Dionysus at Corinth, Teos, Andros, and Elis, wine flowed miraculously from the earth to awe the faithful and enliven festivals.[122] According to the engineer Hero of Alexandria, the door of a tabernacle opened when hot air was channeled from an altar where worshipers burned offerings.[123] In the great sanctuary of Sarapis at Alexandria, the priests used magnetism to move an iron Mars toward a loadstone Venus; in the dim light of the temple, the magnetic attraction was probably aided by wires.[124] In 219, scientists supported the Egyptian state in a religious dispute. At Alexandria, the refugee Spartan king, Cleomenes III, had committed suicide after failing to rally the Alexandrians against Ptolemy IV. The Egyptian king had the Spartan's corpse flayed and exposed in public, but a serpent appeared on or near the body and the populace began to hail the dead man as a god. To quiet the mob and reassure the uneasy Ptolemy, zoologists from the Museum debunked the supernatural aspect of the snake and explained that serpents were generated from decaying marrow and lymph.[125] Seldom has spontaneous generation been so useful to politicians.

The achievements of Hellenistic science raised the stature of scientists in the popular mind. In the *Achaean Woman*, the comic playwright Alexis had a character express great confidence in science:

> Discovery attends on every quest,
> Except for renegades who shirk the toil.
> Now certain men have pushed discovery
> Into the sphere of heaven. Some part they know—
> How planets rise and set and wheel about,
> And of the sun's eclipse. If men have probed
> Worlds far remote, can problems of this earth,
> This common home to which we're born, defy them? [126]

In retrospect, the sanguine hopes of Alexis appear naive because Greek science did little to improve the lives of the peoples of antiquity. While medical advances helped those who could afford treatment, the intellectual activities of mathematicians and astronomers were strictly private pleasures. Even education did not profit much from science. Aratus of Soli composed a verse epitome of astronomical lore, which was admired by Cicero and Saint Paul, but the poet was ignorant of mathematics and observational methods and merely versified an obsolete book by Eudoxus and a mediocre work by Theophrastus. The great popularity of Aratus' *Phaenomena* damaged the quality of general education in the Hellenistic era when most students read his poem as a textbook on astronomy.[127]

Although they were not responsible for the activity of Aratus and other popularizers, leading Hellenistic astronomers endorsed the pseudo-science of astrology. Impossible without mathematical sophistication and an awareness of the proper order of the planets, horoscopic astrology was essentially a product of Greek science.[128] The Platonic astral cult and popular association of celestial bodies with traditional deities had paved the way for the general acceptance of astrology.[129] Even Aristotle sanctioned the belief that the planets were divine beings:

To our forefathers, the planets were gods and nature was a divine order. Later, expediency required that the gods have human or animal shapes to impress the mob. . . . The basic concept that the celestial bodies are divine, is inspired and has survived the cycles of history which have destroyed all the arts and sciences again and again.[130]

Where great men led, lesser men gladly followed.

Only a handful of scientists and philosophers resisted the lure of astral determinism, which explained all human affairs in rational terms. Eudoxus had denounced personal horoscopes, but his views had little effect on Hellenistic intellectuals, and Panaetius was "the only Stoic to reject the prophecies of the astrologers."[131] Few readers of Panaetius were as convinced as Cicero that astrology was a sham. The Roman orator felt that types of divination merely reflected their geographical environments—residents of plains studied the stars, damp climates encouraged weather portents, and nomads observed the flight of birds.[132] Cicero sadly noted that even Democritus was a fervent believer in divination and only Xenophanes and Epicurus rejected the occult art.[133] To the Stoics, fate was an endless chain of causation and astrology was a demonstrable science.[134] In Stoic eyes, a lack of faith in astrology was tantamount to atheism.[135]

A leading Stoic was involved in a major controversy in the history of science. When Aristarchus of Samos published his heliocentric hypothesis, the head of the Stoic school, Cleanthes, denounced the astronomer in a belligerent tract.[136] Cleanthes was inept in scientific matters [137] and launched his polemic under the mistaken impression that heliocentrism would endanger astral determinism.* According to Plutarch,

* Heliocentrism did not dampen Kepler's faith in astrology, and Copernicanism often appeared in an aura of astrology in the sixteenth century.[144]

Cleanthes thought that the Greeks ought to indict Aristarchus of Samos for impiety because he was disturbing the Hearth of the Universe. Aristarchus . . . suggested that the heavens are at rest while the earth is revolving [about the sun] along the ecliptic and rotating on its own axis.[138]

On the basis of this passage, many scholars have given the Stoics credit for suppressing the idea that the earth was not the center of the universe.[139] However, Aristarchus resided at the Museum [139a] and could ignore the fulminations of a dyspeptic philosopher in Athens. Although he was the ancient Copernicus, Aristarchus was not the Galileo of antiquity. The heliocentric system had been suggested only as a hypothesis [140] and was shelved by Hipparchus and other responsible scientists because it conflicted with astronomical observations.[141] Some of the scientific objections (for example, the absence of steller parallax) could be resolved by assuming a cosmos of tremendous distances, but this was unacceptable to scientists who were used to a compact universe. For laymen, of course, the apparent behavior of the sun and moon showed that the earth was central, and Aristarchus' suggestion that the earth was in motion was simply too unsettling. However, Aristarchus may have had one convert. In Seleucid Mesopotamia, the astronomer Seleucus endorsed the notion of a rotating earth and may have accepted the heliocentric view as well.[142] The question of planetary motion was settled by the greatest Hellenistic astronomer, Hipparchus of Nicaea, who elaborated the epicyclic system that would culminate in the grand astronomical synthesis of Claudius Ptolemy.[143]

Although he was a careful and conscientious scientist, Hipparchus embraced astral determinism in his quest for certainty. Pliny the Elder praised the astronomer "who has done more than anyone to prove that man is related to the stars and that our souls are part of the heavens." [145] The attitude of Hipparchus and other Hellenistic scientists toward astrology lent plausibility and respectability to a pseudoscience. According to Martin Nilsson, "the great astrological system, which resembles a gigantic clockwork regulating all things in the universe, the movements of the celestial bodies as well as the events on earth and the fates of man, . . . is an achievement of the Greeks." [146] In the golden age of Greek science, most astronomers capitulated to astrology, which offered the illusory comfort that Providence directed human affairs through astral influences.

Since the stars were responsible for the established order on earth, the subsidized scholars of Alexandria were not likely to question the elevation of astrology to the status of a respectable science. Defended by the greatest astronomers of the era, astrology was entrenched as an exact science, and few men heeded the warning of Epicurus: "It is better to accept the myths of the gods than be slaves to the determinism of the physicists." [147] With regard to astrology, astronomers suspended their critical methodology and followed the practical wisdom of conformity. Hampered by expediency, Hellenistic science resembled Meredith's Lucifer:

> With memory of the old revolt from Awe,
> He reach'd a middle height, and at the stars,
> Which are the brain of heaven, he look'd and sank.
> Around the ancient track march'd, rank on rank,
> The army of unalterable law.

While scientists aided horoscope-mongers, their royal employers joined the ranks of captive kings. The tyrant stars had given the world to Rome.

THREE

The Roman World

SCIENCE AT ROME

Under Roman rule, Greek scientists were respected and well paid, but the new masters of the world were generally indifferent to pure science. The practical Romans were chiefly concerned with applied science and had little patience with theory. A nation of conquerors and administrators, the Romans found medicine and engineering useful, but most viewed pure research as a waste of time. However, no national genius was manifest in Greek theory or Roman practicality. Both nations produced intellectuals, soldiers, and bureaucrats, but Rome arrived late on the scientific scene. When a society adopts an advanced science and technology, its engineers and managers respect the theories behind their equipment, but practical men do not usually have time for contemplation and intellectual adventures. For centuries, Hellenistic technology sufficed for the frontier wars and domestic problems of the Roman world.

Religion was a practical public affair to the Romans who had learned the ancient art of divination from their Etruscan neighbors. Although they boasted of their piety, the leaders of the Roman Republic manipulated auspices with casual indifference. Political expediency dictated the interpretation of omens, and diviners often reversed their opinions to meet the needs of the moment.[1] The conservative Q. Fabius Maximus candidly admitted: "Whatever serves the interests of the Republic has good auspices, and whatever is against the public interest is inauspicious."[2] Since political activity could not take place on festivals or inauspicious days, the official Roman calendar was constantly altered to prevent unwanted legislation.[3] The practical Romans viewed the claims of many astrologers with a jaundiced eye, and in 139 B.C. a praetor expelled from the city those astrologers who were patently dishonest and had prostituted their "science" for profit.[4] However, astrology was a popular fad among Roman intellectuals, and the ruling class of the late Republic often consulted astrologers.

At the close of the first century B.C., the great geographer Strabo of Pontus tried to explode the myth of geographic determinism. He pointed out that Babylonians and Egyptians were scholars because of their training and not as a result of their physical surroundings. Although they shared a common environment, the Athenians and Spartans developed totally different ways of life. According to Strabo, hard lands produced hard men, but governments made their subjects docile and could alter the physical environment to a degree.[5] However, Strabo's views were not shared by the Roman engineer, Vitruvius Pollio, who adapted the geographic notions of Aristotle to justify Roman domination of the Mediterranean world:

The Southern peoples are very intelligent and resourceful in planning . . . but they collapse when courage is required because the sun has sapped their strength. Men born in colder climates are valiant and better suited for battle, but they are dull-witted and have no sense in war. . . . However, Italy is a perfect land . . . lying midway between North and South. With good sense, the Romans smash the courageous barbarians and with valor foil the cunning Southerners. Providence has situated the Roman state in an excellent and temperate region so that Rome could obtain dominion over the whole world.[6]

Apparently, climate and God are always on the side of the victors.

While the ideal life for Greek aristocrats was elegant indolence, the goal of Roman nobles was glory in war and success in politics. Upperclass Romans respected the art of persuasion, but few were attracted to scientific inquiry. Vergil, not Lucretius, was the national poet:

Others, no doubt, will better mould the bronze
To the semblance of soft breathing, draw, from marble,

The living countenance; and others plead
With greater eloquence, or learn to measure,
Better than we, the pathways of the heaven,
The rising of the stars: remember, Roman,
To rule the people under law, to establish
The way of peace, to battle down the haughty,
To spare the meek. Our fine arts, these, forever.[7]

Although Marius scorned Greek military manuals, Polybius had urged Roman generals to be familiar with astronomy and calendrics.[8] Those who heeded his advice were likely dependent on Latin translations of obsolete Hellenistic digests of science. The state did not provide scientific information for the military, but the Senate did order a translation of a Punic manual on agriculture for the benefit of the plantation owners of Italy.[8a] The Carthaginian author, Mago, was highly regarded, and his treatise was often cited by Varro, Columella, and Pliny the Elder. For the most part, Roman nobles received their scientific education from Greek tutors, who had been purchased in the slave mart for less than the price of a good chef.

After the sack of Syracuse in 211, a few scientific instruments were carried off to Rome, where Cicero later saw a planetarium that had been designed by Archimedes to simulate a solar eclipse.[9] Awed by the reputation of the great scientist, Cicero sought out Archimedes' grave in Sicily: "I searched for his resting place which was unknown to the Syracusans who even denied its existence. However, I found the grave covered with brambles and thickets; . . . the stone was inscribed with a sphere and a cylinder." [10] When slaves had cleared away the brush, Cicero paid his respects to Archimedes. The great orator was less enthusiastic when Caesar made a much needed reform in the Roman calendar by establishing the Julian year of 365¼ days in 46 B.C. Cicero growled that the heavens had to obey the dictator.[11] The new calendar caused some confusion even among officials, and the emperor Augustus had to restore order to the Julian year. In the process, he renamed the eighth month August, following the precedent of Caesar who had named the seventh month July.[12] The citizens of Rome had always been casual about time, and the Senate did not employ a water clock to time debates until 159 B.C.[13] Romans were more interested in drains and aqueducts, and the city boasted a splendid sewer system and an excellent water supply. With Roman practicality, Sextus Frontinus contrasted the great aqueducts of the capital with "the idle pyramids and the renowned, but useless, works of the Greeks." [14]

The Romans needed doctors, first to tend wounds and later to treat gout.[15] When Rome was ravaged by plague in 293 B.C., the Senate had sent for the healing god Asclepius. The custodians of Asclepius' shrine at Epidaurus did not wish to part with the deity and gave the Roman envoys another temple snake.[16] Late in the third century, Greek medical science was introduced at Rome but not without opposition. The first public physician at Rome, Archagathus, relied on the knife and the cauterizing iron —his victims nicknamed him "Butcher." The irascible Cato the Elder, who detested all Greeks, was convinced that Hellenic doctors were part of an international conspiracy to murder the people of Rome.[17] However, native medicine was worse than clumsy Greek methods, for Cato believed that dislocated or fractured bones could be set with voodoo.[18] Even the learned Pliny the Elder advised tubercular patients to inhale the smoke of burning dung.[19] Roman medical handbooks were filled with shotgun remedies, magic, and outmoded folklore, and Hellenic medicine was a considerable improvement. However, the Roman public did not abandon its folk remedies, and both ancient magic and Greek medicine were used in the treatment of illness.

Although Marseilles and other cities in Gaul paid physicians well and treated them with respect,[20] the medical profession at Rome was humiliated by the snobbery of the ruling class. Despite his own middle-class origin, Cicero expressed the views of the nobility and was condescending toward professional men: "Society derives much benefit from medicine, architecture, and higher education, but these occupations are only honorable for those men to whose social position such professions are appropriate." [21] Following Cicero's lead, a modern historian has commented: "Art and science were brought to Rome by the more brilliant of her captives and were left wholly in the servile hands." [22] Nevertheless, to attract competent physicians to Rome, the dictator Caesar bestowed Roman citizenship on aliens who practiced medicine in the capital.[23] The hopelessly ill still made use of Asclepius, and the emperor Claudius decreed that slaves, who had been abandoned in the sanctuary as incurable, were to be freed if healed by the god.[24] Claudius' policy encouraged owners to provide better medical care for their slaves.

In the Imperial period, the social status of professional men improved as the ruling class gradually evolved into an aristocracy of merit. At the courts of Augustus and Tiberius, royal physicians received handsome salaries, 250,000 sesterces a year.[25] Claudius paid twice as much to his personal physician, Xenophon of Cos, and exempted the doctor's home city from taxation because of the contributions that Cos had made to medical progress. However, Xenophon did not take his professional ethics seriously, for he helped the empress Agrippina murder Claudius. When the emperor vomited the poisonous mushrooms which Agrippina had served him, Xenophon killed Claudius with an enema of colocynth.[26] Most prominent doctors were graduates of the great medical schools of the East,[27] and a degree from the medical institute at Alexandria guaranteed its holder a lucrative career.[28] Able physicians received wealth and gratitude from their communities. In Asia Minor, the city of Adada inscribed public honors for "Orestes, son of Antiochus, who chose to learn the science of medicine and died in Alexandria."[29] At Rome, the emperor Vespasian paid professors of literature 100,000 sesterces a year, and later Domitian presented a scholar with income property of equal value.[30] Vespasian also exempted physicians from taxation, but Domitian withdrew the privilege from doctors who taught their skills to slaves.[31] The emperors Hadrian and Antoninus Pius released physicians from obligatory state service, but the exemption was effective only at the doctor's official place of residence or at Rome, "everybody's home town."[32] In the early third century A.D., the emperor Severus Alexander was generous to teachers of literature, medicine, engineering, astrology, and architecture: "He paid professors regular salaries, supplied them with lecture rooms, and provided food for freeborn students who were poor."[33] However, accounts of Severus Alexander's reign are riddled with propaganda, and his aid to education may have been exaggerated.

In the field of technology, the Roman state intervened twice to suppress inventions which seemed detrimental to the public good. During the reign of Tiberius, "a flexible glass was invented, but the workshop of the inventor was completely destroyed for fear that copper, silver, and gold would lose value." [34] Although the flexibility of the glass is doubtful,[35] the destruction of the workshop was consistent with the personality of Tiberius, who was preoccupied with monetary problems and often took drastic action to prevent financial crises.[36] The genial emperor Vespasian handled a troublesome invention with better grace:

An engineer devised a new machine which could haul large pillars . . . at little expense. However, Vespasian rejected the invention and asked, "Who will take care of my poor?" Nevertheless, the emperor paid the inventor a handsome fee.[37]

To Vespasian, employment for the masses had priority over progress in automation. Despite these two episodes, the Roman government had little interest in technology, except for the military. In the imperial period, water wheels were used for grinding grain, and Gallic farmers employed harvesting machines.[38] However, these improvements were private enterprises and not the result of any concern by the state for science or economic development.

To the subsidized scholars at the Museum and privileged professions throughout the empire, the emperors of Rome were remote figures. Nevertheless, a few scientists stood close to the throne and assisted the Roman rulers in the formulation of policy. Since astrology was accepted as a science by the majority of educated men, every emperor in the first century A.D. relied upon his court astrologers for insights into the future. Like the diviners of the past, the court astrologers were shrewd men and well informed on domestic and foreign affairs as well as proficient in astronomy and mathematics. Astrologers and their patrons considered a false prophecy an error in calculation and never lost faith in the scientific nature of astrology.[39] * Because ambitious politicians also consulted astrologers, Roman rulers worried that favorable horoscopes might encourage conspiracies against the regime. The emperors tried to curb the general prac-

* A modern analogy would be a rocket failure which may ruin a career but destroys no one's belief in space vehicles.

tice of astrology and often expelled private astrologers from Rome. In 11 A.D., Augustus decreed that no prophecy should be delivered without witnesses or concern death. To relieve the public's curiosity about his own fate, the aged emperor published the astrological details of his birth.[40] Later restrictions on the private use of astrology followed the precedent of Augustus' edict, but his successors did not reveal their personal horoscopes to the general public.

As scientists and advisers, the Roman court astrologers are comparable to the scientific consultants who help shape national policy in the twentieth century. Like modern scientists, the imperial astrologers frequented "the corridors of power." The historian Tacitus commented acidly on the astrologers: "Such men mislead the powerful and deceive the ambitious, practicing a profession which in our country will always be outlawed and always maintained." [41] The careers of Tiberius Claudius Thrasyllus and his son Balbillus reveal the power available to scientists who wished to play the grim game of politics. Thrasyllus was a learned Alexandrian astrologer who had met the future emperor Tiberius on Rhodes. Because Thrasyllus prophesied Tiberius' succession to the throne, the emperor became addicted to astrology and depended on Thrasyllus for the rest of his life.[42] At court, Thrasyllus headed the clique of astrologers and intellectuals who surrounded Tiberius and later followed him to his retreat on Capri. Thrasyllus' granddaughter Ennia married the wily Macro who became the praetorian prefect after the fall of Tiberius' chief aide, Sejanus. Macro played on the morbid suspicions of Tiberius who lived in fear of conspiracy, but Thrasyllus reassured the aged emperor that he had another decade of life. Relieved by the astrologer's lie, Tiberius did not unleash the purge that he had planned against Caligula and others who might profit from his death.[43] Apparently, Thrasyllus also persuaded Tiberius not to exclude Caligula from the succession.[44] The great astrologer died before his patron and left the old emperor disconsolate. Fortunately, Thrasyllus did not witness the intrigues of Caligula, who seduced Ennia. Through her, Caligula won the aid of the unsuspecting Macro in the struggles over the imperial succession. Although he had secretly promised to make her his empress, Caligula turned on Ennia and her husband after the death of Tiberius. Having no further need of the pair, the new emperor ordered Ennia and Macro to commit suicide.[45] However, the tragedy of Ennia did not darken the star of the house of Thrasyllus.

The success of Thrasyllus had been due to his good sense and high reputation as an astrologer. Tiberius Claudius Balbillus followed his father's lead and became a skillful astrologer under Caligula's successor Claudius. A close friend and adviser of the emperor, Balbillus served Claudius as a diplomat and as an educational director in Egypt. At court, the ambitious astrologer participated in the intrigues surrounding Claudius' choice of an heir. Supporting the empress Agrippina, Balbillus supplied glowing prophecies for young Nero, her son by a prior marriage.[46] When Claudius adopted Nero as heir, Balbillus was rewarded with the lucrative governorship of Egypt.[47] After the death of Claudius, the agile astrologer became a confidant of the emperor Nero. With astrological arguments, Balbillus defended the bloody purges that characterized Nero's regime.[48] Eventually eclipsed by the astrologers of the empress Poppaea, Balbillus was forced to withdraw from the dangerous court of Nero. After the overthrow of the tyrant, Balbillus became the astrological adviser of the emperor Vespasian, who expelled private astrologers from Rome.[49] Although Vespasian was not afraid to employ men whose horoscopes foretold future greatness, his suspicious son Domitian slew such individuals as threats to his throne.[50] The future emperor Nerva survived only because an astrologer assured Domitian that he would outlive Nerva. Under the emperor Trajan, Balbillus' grandson, C. Julius Antiochus Epiphanes Philopappus, was appointed to the high office of the consulship in 109 A.D.[51] The family of Thrasyllus had reached impressive heights by combining repute as scientists with political acumen.

The success of Thrasyllus and Balbillus took place in a world where astrology was respected and dissent was dangerous. The emperors had replaced the turbulent inefficiency of the Republic with the awful simplicity of autocracy. Most Romans in government preferred the quiet anonymity of a bureaucratic career and only raised their voices to praise the reigning monarch. Under Augustus, Asinius Pollio had abandoned politics to write history but could not be frank about recent events: "I keep quiet, for it is not wise to write against a man who has the power to purge." [52] Like Stalin, Augustus was accepted as an authority on subjects other than politics. The emperor decided that Caesar's poems lacked merit, and the works vanished from the state libraries.[53] When the historian Livy was faced with an antiquarian problem, Augustus inspected a temple and uncovered ancient evidence which solved Livy's dilemma and also discomforted a political enemy.[54] According to Sir Ronald Syme, "the opportune discovery of important documents in sacred edifices tends to happen when political morality and paleographic science are at a low level." [55] In 12 A.D., Augustus conducted a search for subversive literature, burned offensive books, and hounded their authors.[56] Under Tiberius, intellectual repression continued, but the whimsical Caligula restored a few books that had been banned by Augustus and Tiberius.[57] When Domitian burned the works of his critics, the historian Tacitus observed that the despot hoped that "the voice of the Roman people . . . and the conscience of mankind were consumed in the flames." [58] However, Tacitus and his colleagues in the Senate did not protest until after the death of Domitian.[59] In Imperial Rome, conformity was a virtue and discretion became a habit.

With colossal finality, Rome had embraced order at all cost. The Roman empire commanded enormous resources and was not indifferent to science. However, science did not blossom in the shadow of the Caesars as it had in the gaudy days of the Ptolemies. To Pliny the Elder, the stalemate in science seemed a paradox. When the Greeks had been divided into warring nations and pirates had infested the seas, research had flourished and great advances were made in science. Yet in the enlightened reign of Vespasian, science was at a standstill although travel was safe and access to books was easy. Pliny concluded that, while Hellenic scientists of the past had been motivated by a desire to expand man's knowledge of the universe, his own contemporaries were preoccupied with security and wealth.[60] The courtier Petronius too felt that astronomers had succumbed to the lure of cash.[61] The slack in science had a parallel in the field of rhetoric where, according to Tacitus, servility had silenced eloquence.[62] In the second century, the orator Aelius

Aristides expressed the mood of the educated class with a chilling phrase: "No other way of life is left." [63] At Delphi, even the oracle of Apollo avoided controversy and adopted a careful banality.[64] In the awesome stillness of the Roman Peace, scientists struck no discordant note.

In the ancient world, medicine and religion were always close. For the poor, temple cures were cheaper than professional medical care, and for the desperately ill, divine aid was the ultimate recourse. According to Kerényi:

First, the school of physicians at Kos achieved a high level of medical science; next, a turn toward religious depth, originating at Epidaurus, spread to Kos itself; finally, in the early imperial age, the medical element regained its predominance, even at Epidaurus.[65]

However, Epidaurus remained the Lourdes of antiquity, and the shrine was hung with replicas of parts of the body which patients believed had been cured by Asclepius.[66] In his handbook for tourists of Greece, Pausanias recommended a visit to Epidaurus and described the famous sanitarium as crawling with sacred snakes.[67] Throughout the Roman empire, incurable or pious patients slept in the temples of Asclepius and other gods and hoped to be visited and cured by the deities in dreams.[68]

The attitude of the age was reflected in its greatest doctor, Galen, who believed that Asclepius visited him in dreams. Although many Hellenistic physicians had rejected the Hippocratic doctrine of humors, Galen endorsed the four humors, for he felt that the microcosm of the body was a model of the macrocosm of the universe. While Providence maintained order among earth, air, fire, and water in the cosmos, the soul presided over a balance of blood, phlegm, yellow bile, and black bile in the healthy body. The great doctor also believed in sympathetic magic and astrology.[69] In dissecting beasts, Galen found evidence of divine order and "looked for God in the entrails of animals." [70] As a religious man, Galen was particularly critical of the atomists:

Some of these people have even expressly declared that the soul possesses no reasoning faculty, but that we are led like cattle by the impression of our senses. . . . In their view, obviously, courage, wisdom, temperance, and self-control are all mere nonsense, we do not love either each other or our offspring, nor do the gods care anything for us. This school also despises dreams, birds, omens, and the whole of astrology. . . . [But, the atomic approach is wrong because] there is a consensus in the movements of air and fluid throughout the whole body. Nature acts throughout in an artistic and equitable manner.[71]

Piety did not lessen the practical skills of Galen who served as a court physician for Marcus Aurelius, Commodus, and Septimius Severus. For Marcus Aurelius, Galen prepared daily doses of narcotics which helped the Stoic emperor endure his imperial bondage.[72] Because of Galen's great repute and prodigious writings, his theories were widely accepted in late antiquity. In the Dark Ages, some knowledge of Galen was preserved in Italy, but generally his works were unknown in the West.[72a] However, Byzantine physicians revered Galen, as did Near Eastern Christians who translated his works into Syriac. Arabic scholars took up the study of Galen with enthusiasm. When the Arabic versions of his works were translated into Latin in the eleventh and twelfth centuries, Galen became the medical canon of the Middle Ages. Both Muslims and Christians admired Galen's knowledge of medicine and responded to his religious orientation.

In the second century, the craze for astrology continued unabated. Although the famous rhetorician Favorinus of Arles criticized the claims of astrology, his patron Hadrian was not convinced, for the emperor was addicted to the art.[73] In the reign of Marcus Aurelius, the astrological hack Vettius Valens complained because the regime was unsympathetic to astrology:

This fills me with resentment and with envy of those ancient kings and despots who were enthusiasts for the science. Why did I not have the good fortune to live in those spacious days and to breathe the fresh air of their spiritual freedom for research? . . . At the present day the effective investigation of facts is obscured and blighted by fear.[74]

Valens was probably referring to the brief ban on astrologers which Marcus Aurelius had decreed during the rebellion of Avidius Cassius.[75] Although he harassed subversive astrologers,

Marcus Aurelius fined the city of Nicaea for neglecting the memory of Hipparchus, the master of astronomy and astrology.[76]

The famous astronomer Claudius Ptolemy was also an accomplished astrologer. His synthesis of Greek astronomy was "one of the greatest masterpieces of scientific analysis ever written." [77] Employing the epicycles and eccentrics of Hipparchus, the Ptolemaic system satisfied an intellectual clientele who believed that the physical world agreed with the laws of mathematics. For Ptolemy, the study of astronomy was a rich spiritual experience:

> Mortal though I be, yea ephemeral, if but a moment
> I gaze up at the night's starry domain of heaven,
> Then no longer on earth I stand; I touch the Creator,
> And my lively spirit drinketh immortality.[78]

Since the heavens revealed a divine presence, Ptolemy employed his science to demonstrate that celestial bodies influenced mankind. To Ptolemy, astral determinism seemed as demonstrable as the laws of genetics are to moderns. Dismissing irrelevant individual factors, Ptolemy insisted that "both in general and in particular whatever events depend upon a first cause, which is irresistible and more powerful than anything that opposes it, must by all means take place." [79] Like the decrees of Rome, the mandates of the stars were inescapable.

Surveying a world dominated by the stars and Rome, Ptolemy concluded that "weaker natures always yield to the stronger, and the particular always falls under the general." [80] According to Ptolemy, national characteristics were determined by the planets and the zodiac. Thus, Mesopotamians studied mathematics and astronomy (Virgo and Mercury) and Greeks were noble and independent (Mars), liberty-loving and democratic (Jupiter), and fond of music, learning, and letters (Venus and Mercury). While Semites were commercial, unscrupulous, despicable, cowardly, treacherous, servile, and fickle (Sagittarius and Mercury), Egyptians were close to the Sun and the Zodiac and were shrewd, inventive, versed in divine lore, mathematical, masculine, and honest—(Ptolemy was either a Greek Egyptian or an Egyptian Greek). Because of Aries and Mars, the Jews were

atheists and rebels, but Leo and the Sun made Italians coopera-
tive, benevolent, and masterful.[81] As an apologist for Roman
dominion, Ptolemy adapted the "science" of astrology to suit
the anti-Semitic prejudices of the emperors. His ethnic determinism was essentially an astral variant of the geographic notions of Aristotle and Vitruvius. In justifying "the ways of God
to men," the great astronomer reflected the dictates of Roman
policy.

SCIENCE AND SURVIVAL

In *The Golden Bough*, Sir James Frazer depicted the historical process whereby magic is replaced by religious myth:

In magic, man depends on his own strength to meet the difficulties
and dangers that beset him on every side. He believes in a certain
established order of nature on which he can surely count, and which
he can manipulate for his own ends. When he discovers his mistakes,
when he recognizes sadly that both the order of nature which he had
assumed and the control which he had believed himself to exercise
over it were purely imaginary, he ceases to rely on his own intelligence and his own unaided efforts and throws himself humbly on
the mercy of certain great invisible beings behind the veil of nature,
to whom he now ascribes all those far-reaching powers which he once
arrogated to himself. Thus, in the acuter minds, magic is gradually
superseded by religion, which explains the succession of natural phenomena as regulated by the will, the passion, or the caprice of spiritual beings like man in kind, though vastly superior to him in power.[82]

If he had substituted "science" for "magic," Frazer's formula
would have described the triumph of religion over science which
characterized the intellectual mood of late antiquity. A similar
miasma is likely to occur if the modern world would undergo
large-scale nuclear wars—the survivors would decry science and
its works and raise up dark, new gods.

In the second century, ancient science had capitulated with
Ptolemy's defense of astrology and Galen's surrender to the
supernatural. Is this a fair charge? Astrology was the all-pervad-
ing natural law of the Greco-Roman world and indeed of Europe
before Newton,[83] and even magic was gingerly regarded as a
semiscience. But, respectability is a poor criterion by which to

assess ideas, for divination too was once venerable and practiced by learned men. Unlike phlogiston, astrology and supernaturalism were not merely erroneous views of the universe—they had religious components and opened the door to the mindless world of the occult. Newtonian science can be accepted without endorsing the whimsical notions of Newton on Biblical prophecy, but the world view of Ptolemy included astrology as an integral part, and Galen embraced mysticism and even magic. Both Ptolemy and Galen were giants of science and deserving of respect, but they were also allies of occultism, and their great prestige reinforced the growing irrationality of late antique thought. When the Roman empire was threatened by internal crises and foreign invaders, the tempo of religiosity increased, and science did not halt the retreat from reason.

In the third century, a religious climate pervaded all levels of society, and "powerful court circles listened with attention to the ravings of Asiatic theosophists." [84] The Severan dynasty was especially addicted to astrology. Before he became emperor, Septimius Severus had chosen Julia Domna as his wife because she had an imperial horoscope.[85] Philosophers too were in tune with the invisible world and were drawn to occultism. The great Neoplatonist Plotinus disdained astrology but enlivened séances with spirit effluences.[86] Deeply impressed by Plotinus, the emperor Gallienus wished to build a city for philosophers to be called Platonopolis, but jealous courtiers opposed the project.[87] Although the city of sages was stillborn, the Christian community expanded in the troubled third century, and "the gap between Christianity and science was narrowing as Christian learning advanced and antique science declined." [88]

A few converts to Christianity were well versed in science, and Bishop Anatolius of Alexandria, a former Peripatetic, wrote on astronomy and arithmetic.[89] However, there were obvious problems for Christians in the confrontation of science with revelation. The historian Eusebius quoted a religious polemic against a group of second-century Christians at Rome who had been accused of heresy:

They abandon the holy works of God and study geometry, for they are of the earth and speak of the earth and know nothing of Him who comes from above. Some of them study the geometry of Euclid and admire Aristotle and Theophrastus. Some of them almost worship Galen. To justify their heresy, they use the arts of unbelievers and weaken the simple truth of the holy scriptures with godless cunning. It goes without saying that they are far from the faith.[90]

However, not many Christians were in danger of losing faith through excessive familiarity with science.

Although the church was defended by articulate and even learned men, the doctrines of Christianity were not demonstrable in terms of logic—even the faithful could not agree on such esoteric matters as the Trinity. Moreover, the problems of science were not compelling issues to Christians, who were sometimes persecuted by the Roman state and might be called upon to endure agonies for their faith. The composition of matter and the position of the stars were not important to men who were anxious to escape the physical world and many of whom expected its imminent destruction. The overwhelming majority of Christians were simple folk who were concerned with salvation and would agree with Milton's counsel:

> Heav'n is for thee too high
> To know what passes there; be lowlie wise:
> Think onely what concernes thee and thy being;
> Dream not of other Worlds. . . .

From the point of view of most Christians, science was in league with the high and the mighty, who rejected the Gospel and slaughtered saints.

In the third and fourth centuries, the Roman empire was assaulted by aggressive foreign enemies and internally torn by mutinies and peasant revolts. Late in the third century, the emperor Diocletian mobilized the empire into a totalitarian state in order that Roman society might survive. A zealous administrator, Diocletian believed in the effect of edicts and wielded the pen more than the sword. When he suppressed a rebellion in Egypt in 296, the emperor also ordered a wholesale destruction of Egyptian books on alchemy. According to a confused Byzantine source:

Because of the revolutions, Diocletian treated the Egyptians harshly and cruelly and having sought out the books written by their forefathers on the chemistry of gold and silver, burned them lest wealth should accrue to the Egyptians through this art and lest they emboldened by riches should in the future revolt against the Romans.[91]

More likely, the alchemists had used their skills in gold and silver plating to counterfeit coins and undermine Diocletian's currency. If he had believed that the Egyptians could actually produce precious metals, the emperor would have enlisted their services in filling his own treasuries.

Like most emperors, Diocletian feared the subversive aspects of astrology and tried to suppress the art with an empire-wide ban, but his efforts were not successful. Under Constantine, astrology still flourished, but Firmicus Maternus warned his fellow astrologers:

Be careful never to give an answer to anyone inquiring about the life of the Roman emperor. For it is neither necessary nor permitted for us to learn anything concerning the state of the realm through nefarious curiosity. But anyone who when asked says anything about the fate of the emperor is both a criminal and worthy of every punishment.[92]

Late in the fourth century, the Christian emperor Valentinian I decreed that both teachers and students of astrology were guilty of a capital crime.[93] However, the collapse of general education after the barbarian invasions did more to eradicate astrology in the West than all the edicts of worried emperors.

In late antiquity, the Roman empire was beset by marauding barbarians in Europe and menaced by Persia in the East. Too often, the emperors were preoccupied with military affairs to the exclusion of domestic reforms. Over the centuries, Rome had frequently modified tactics and adopted new weapons until Ammianus Marcellinus could boast in the fourth century of missiles, filled with naphtha and inflammable oils, and long-range projectiles which fell upon an enemy before he was aware that Romans were in the vicinity.[94] In the past, the emperors took comfort in the fact that the barbarians of Europe possessed a primitive technology at best. The historian Tacitus had remarked complacently: "Barbarians are ignorant of military engines and the management of sieges, while we Romans excel in such matters." [95] Unfortunately, no nation conforms to its stereotype for long, and the barbaric enemies of Christian Rome had adequate military equipment and even hired mercenary specialists. When the Visigoths crossed the Hellespont on rafts in 400, the Byzantine historian Zosimus was astonished by "the inventiveness of barbarians." [96] A century later, the Huns would devise a battering ram that was superior to Byzantine or Persian rams.[97] In short, the much-despised barbarians were both imitative and inventive. The historian of technology, Lynn White, Jr., notes that the clever barbarians of Europe invented trousers, felt, skis, barrels, tubs, soap, and the heavy plow.[98] When the barbarians attacked the northern frontiers of the empire in the fourth century, Rome needed desperately to improve its weaponry to regain military superiority.

During the reign of Valentinian I, the unknown author of *De Rebus Bellicis* proposed to meet the crisis with new inventions and social reform:

In the technical arts (among which we include the invention of weapons) progress is due not to those of the highest birth or immense wealth or public office or eloquence derived from literary studies but solely to men of intellectual power. . . . [The barbarians] are by no means considered strangers to mechanical inventiveness where nature comes to their assistance.

However, the Roman ruling class was mainly concerned with the accumulation of wealth:

This store of gold meant that the houses of the powerful were crammed full and their splendor enhanced to the destruction of the poor, the poorer classes of course being held down by force. But the poor were driven by their afflictions into various criminal enterprises, and losing sight of all respect for law, all feeling of loyalty, they entrusted their revenge to crime. For they often inflicted the most severe injuries on the Empire, laying waste the fields, breaking the peace with outbursts of brigandage, stirring up animosities, and passing from one crime to another, supported usurpers.[99]

The rising of the masses, who had been submerged by poverty, revealed the immediate need for economic and social reform, and the military threat required new inventions.

To eliminate oppressive taxes and waste, the author of *De Rebus Bellicis* recommended a tax reduction for peasants and an end to corruption among government officials. He also proposed that the frontiers of the empire be fortified and that Roman armies employ scythed chariots, better artillery, and a warship with paddle wheels which were powered by oxen on treadmills. The novel vessel would have been the only ship before Fulton that was independent of the wind or human muscle power.[100] Although Valentinian was interested in inventions,[101] the tract *De Rebus Bellicis* never reached the eyes of the emperor or responsible officials. Probably, its criticism of the upper class offended courtiers and discouraged bureaucrats from supporting the proposals for new weapons. In the field of technology, Rome coasted on its oars until repeated defeats demonstrated that the major distinction between Roman and barbarian military science was semantic.

In the eastern provinces of the Roman empire, great centers of learning still flourished, but science was no longer a beacon for the intelligentsia. While late antiquity produced some distinguished mathematicians, mathematics was a safe subject that was not involved in religious controversy. Although Greek science leveled off rather than declined under Roman rule,[102] the spiritual malaise of the third and fourth century undermined respect for science among the educated classes. Science was barely tolerated in an atmosphere where magic and mystery were defended by the authority of the state. Not the scientist but the priest, the soldier, and the bureaucrat were the pillars of society. In the fourth century, the historian Ammianus Marcellinus noted the intellectual anemia of the Alexandrian schools:

The teachers of the arts show signs of life, and the geometrical measuring-rod brings to light whatever is concealed. The stream of music is not yet wholly dried up among them, harmony is not reduced to silence. The consideration of the motion of the universe and of the stars is still kept warm with some, few though they be, and there are others who are skilled in numbers; and a few besides are versed in the knowledge which reveals the course of the fates.[103]

Ammianus' comment is a pitiful epitaph for the city which had once been the intellectual marvel of the world.[103a]

The ultimate fate of the Alexandrian libraries is a dismal tale. In the late fourth century Christian mobs sacked public buildings in Alexandria and burned many books. Augustine's protégé Orosius mentioned that smashed book chests could still be seen in 416.[104] Many books which survived Christian bigotry were burned in 646 by command of the Khalif 'Umar after the second fall of Alexandria. According to legend, the Khalif had decided that all books other than the Quran were either false or superfluous.[105] Not all the books burned by Christians and Muslims were of irreplaceable value.* Despite research in medicine and mathematics, Alexandria had declined under a cloud of pedantry and piety, and the Museum had ceased creative activity in most fields of knowledge. Contrary to cabalistic lore, words possess no magical vitality, and books are feeble aids without questioning minds and a passion for discovery.

The decay of ancient learning was of little consequence to the majority of Christians. Even educated Christians were ambivalent toward science, and many of the faithful were frankly hostile. The classic Christian attack on science had been made by the eloquent Tertullian in the second century:

What has Athens to do with Jerusalem, the Academy with the Church? . . . We have no need for curiosity since Jesus Christ, nor for inquiry since the Evangel. . . . It was highly appropriate that Thales, while his eyes were roaming the heavens in astronomical observation, should have tumbled into a well. This mishap may well serve to illustrate the fate of all who occupy themselves with the stupidities of philosophy. . . . It is not to thee that I address myself, the soul which, formed in the schools, trained in the libraries, belches forth a fund of academic wisdom, but thee, the simple and uncultivated soul, such as they have who have nothing else, whose whole experience has been gleaned on street corners and crossroads and in the industrial plant. I need thine inexperience. . . . It is the "secret deposit of congenital and inborn knowledge" which contains the truth, and this is not a product of secular discipline. The soul comes before letters, words before books, and man himself before the philosopher and the poet.[106]

* In the words of Robert Hillyer:
    Far better Alexandria in flames
    Than buried beneath unimportant names.

Despite his fulminations, Tertullian was well-read in secular literature.

In the third century, the author of the tract *Didascalia Apostolorum* warned Christians against contact with pagan learning:

Avoid all books of the heathen. For what hast thou to do with strange sayings or laws or lying prophecies which also turn away from the faith them that are young . . . ? If thou wouldst read historical narratives, thou hast the Book of Kings; but if philosophers and wise men, thou hast the Prophets. . . . But if thou wouldst read of the beginning of the world, thou hast the Genesis of the great Moses. . . . All strange writings therefore which are contrary to these wholly eschew.[107]

The militancy and ignorance of such diatribes were repeated by the Christian Arnobius Afer in the fourth century:

What is it to you . . . to examine, to investigate . . . whether the sun is larger than the earth or measures only a foot across; whether the moon shines by the light of another or by its own beams? There is no gain in knowing these things. . . . Leave these things to God.[108]

When he was converted to Christianity, the astrologer Firmicus Maternus became a zealous bigot and begged the state to extirpate paganism with fire and sword.[109] Even great minds succumbed to spiritual weariness and turned against science. Augustine of Hippo, a former professor, declared his faith in pious ignorance: "A good man who clings to Thee, although he does not even know the circles of the Great Bear, is better than an astronomer who can measure the heavens and number the stars but is forgetful of Thee." [110] Like Tertullian, Saint Augustine was a professional scholar and well-read in the classics that he now disdained. However, most Christians knew little of science and the secular learning that churchmen denounced.

Unfortunately for the intellectual development of Europe, the Christian canon included the Old Testament, wherein Hebrew writers had preserved the outmoded cosmology of the Mesopotamian box universe. In general, Greek science viewed the earth as a sphere around which the sun, moon, and planets orbited; the whole system was surrounded at a great distance by the sphere of fixed stars. To the Hebrews, on the other hand, the inhabited earth was the flat bottom of a box, the top of which was a solid sky; above and below the box world was water. Genesis 1.7 flatly stated that God "separated the waters which were under the firmament from the waters which were above the firmament"; and Exodus 7.11 explained the flood of Noah with the same notion: "All the fountains of the great deep burst forth, and the windows of the heavens were opened." [111] Job 22.14 and 37.18 assert that the sky is a solid roof,[112] and Isaiah 40.22 confirms the chamberlike nature of the world: God "stretches out the heavens like a curtain and spreads them like a tent to dwell in." Many Greek scientists believed in the existence of antipodes, a race of men who inhabited the southern hemisphere, but the apostle Paul claimed that the Gospel had been preached "to the ends of the earth" in his lifetime.[113] Christian literalists viewed Paul's remark as a denial of the antipodes. Thus, to many of the faithful, the concepts of a spherical earth and antipodal humans clashed with the scriptures which Christians espoused.

In the fourth century, the battle between science and scripture began with a withering blast by the Christian apologist, Lactantius, who ridiculed the antipodes as a false idea based on the absurd assumption of a spherical earth.[114] Lynn Thorndike felt that Lactantius "should hardly be cited as typical of early Christian attitudes in such matters," [115] but Lactantius was atypical only in the brashness of his attack. With more finesse, the Cappadocian bishop Basil noted that scientists had disagreed on the shape of the earth—some had thought it a disc, others a cylinder, others a sphere—but Moses had said nothing about such topics which were simply unnecessary for salvation.[116] Bishop Ambrose of Milan, who based his *Hexameron* on Basil's work, was equivocal about the waters above the sky, but he agreed with the Eastern bishop that the size or shape of the earth were vain matters unworthy of Moses' attention.[117] Ambrose's friend Augustine hesitated to assert the sphericity of the earth, but he once held, like Origen, that the celestial waters were not literal but stood for angelic beings.[118] Later, Augustine retracted this daring view,[119] and his general position on science and scripture was typical of Christianity in his time: "The words of Scripture have more authority than the most exalted human intellect." [120] Even in the Dark Ages, an occasional Christian like Bede would assert the spherical shape of the earth, but most Christians felt that the idea was erroneous and ungodly because it contradicted Holy Writ.[121] If educated men such as Lactantius and Augustine sacrificed scientific to scriptural authority, how feeble must have been the hold of science on the minds of the illiterate mass of Christians. The pagans of late antiquity had no qualms over scripture, but they too were enmeshed in the supernaturalism and superstitions of the age.

Since the conversion of the emperor Constantine, Christian bigots could rely on the support of the state in their constant quarrels with opponents. As long as education and tolerance prevailed, Christian gibes at the limitations of reason were legitimate protests among intellectuals. However, antirationalism became a battle cry for Christian fanatics who sacked libraries and burned pagan books. In 415, a Christian mob at Alexandria murdered the pagan mathematician and philosopher, Hypatia, who was one of the few women to attain intellectual prominence in antiquity.[122] The Roman state, too, intervened in religious controversy, and the wrath of Christian emperors was directed against both pagans and dissenting Christians. In 527, the Byzantine emperor Justinian barred pagans and heretics from academic appointments and confiscated their property and endowments.[123] On the authority of Justinian's decree, the venerable Platonic Academy was closed in 529 and many of its members fled to the court of Chosroes I of Persia. In 532, the magnanimous Persian king arranged for the homesick scholars to return to Athens on condition that Justinian would not force them to accept Christianity.[124] Defenseless in a total society, scientists and scholars had no recourse when the Byzantine state demanded the final gesture of conformity.

While Christian learning continued in Byzantium, Western Europe languished under barbarous chiefs who were encamped in the ruins of Britain, Gaul, Spain, and Italy. Five centuries would elapse before urban civilization revived in the West. Since Medieval humanists looked with disdain on the barbaric antics of their ancestors, Petrarch labeled the era between the fourth and fourteenth century as the "Dark Ages." [125] While few moderns would extend the Dark Ages to the eve of the Reformation, romantic admirers of Medievalism are often embarrassed by the condition of intellectual life in Western Europe before the eleventh century. For the historian of science, the Dark Ages is an appropriate term for the period following the fall of Rome, because Western Europe was blanketed with barbarism and general illiteracy. The preservation of a few meager shoots of ancient knowledge did not alter the pattern of cultural regression which followed the collapse of urban society in the West. When the habits of civilization were arrested by the barbarian invasions of the fifth century, books and baths were no longer considered necessities by the peoples of the West.

Occasionally, history is enlivened by episodes that are symbolic as well as dramatic. In the sixth century, the Roman philosopher and politician, Boethius, hoped to preserve the classics of Greek science in Latin translations, but he only completed a few works on arithmetic, music, and logic.* Boethius was also a trusted official at the court of Theodoric, the Gothic king of Italy. Unfortunately for the development of science, Boethius became involved in the religio-political intrigues of the emperor Justinian who intended to recover Italy for the Byzantine empire. Suspecting a far-reaching conspiracy among the senatorial class, Theodoric ordered the execution of Boethius and his father-in-law. The unfortunate scholar was tortured and clubbed to death in 524.[126] The ignominious death of Boethius was precisely the fate which earlier scholars and scientists had sought to escape by time-serving and avoiding politics.

The irony of Boethius' death was heightened by the fact that the king who executed him was illiterate; he could not even sign his own name. Theodoric had to endorse documents by tracing the letters "legi" with the aid of a golden stencil.[127] Another contemporary sovereign, the Byzantine emperor Justin, who rose from humble beginnings, was also illiterate and needed a stencil to endorse official papers.[128] If the two rulers had been literate and interested in cosmology, they could have read an interesting exercise in Christian science by the monk Cosmas Indicopleus-

* His friend, Cassiodorus, directed a similar project but produced works chiefly of ecclesiastical interest. The secular knowledge preserved by Cassiodorus was inadequate to brighten a darkening age.

tes, who propounded the intriguing idea that the world was shaped like the Ark of the Covenant and that angels provided motor power for the planets. In the words of a Marxist critic, "angels rushed in where fools had feared to tread." [129] More than time and religion separated the age of Theodoric, Justin, and Cosmas from the era of Marcus Aurelius, Galen, and Claudius Ptolemy. In the hope of survival, the Romans had placed their trust in militarism and religion, but Rome fell and civilization disintegrated. In its heyday, the Roman empire had not appreciated the scientific spirit and valued only the applied sciences. However, there was no safety in technology when the barbarians availed themselves of the same techniques.

In the ruins of the Roman world, the holy simpleton became an ideal for sensitive men. Although Christian antirationalism contributed to the demise of the scientific spirit, pagan intellectuals had already surrendered to the invisible world. When intelligent men take up séances and fear "things that go bump in the night," science must suffer even though knowledge is preserved in some fields. If society had not been eroded by irrationalism, ancient science would not have been destroyed by the barbarian invasions and the looting of libraries. There are generations who will not suffer a witch to live, and others who will watch science die with equanimity. No science, however advanced, will continue to progress or even survive when the society sustaining it collapses or becomes obsessed with other matters. Truth, crushed to earth, stays there.

ICARUS

According to Aristotle, "a lover of myths is in a sense a lover of wisdom, for myths are composed of wonders." [130] Wondrous things worry men and make them puzzle over the meaning of phenomena. In the dim world of legend, the craftsman Daedalus mastered nature without understanding it. With the skills of experience, Daedalus created wax wings for his son and hoped that Icarus would soar out of reach of the tyrant Minos. But Icarus ignored his father's warning and placed too much trust in the artificial wings. He flew too high and exposed the invention to the heat of the sun. When the wings collapsed, Icarus plunged to his death while Daedalus went on to serve a despot in the West. Icarus fell because of his confidence in an invention and his careless disregard of the limitations of man. The myth suggests that man does not become a god just because he is clever enough to fly.

In the ancient world, the craftsman survived as mechanic, leech, and engineer, serving all who would pay for his skills. However, science, like Icarus, rose on wings made by craftsmen, soared spectacularly, and fell. The legendary Icarus disobeyed his father, and scientists did not learn from the experience of craftsmen. A king might hire a man, but he could not command his craft. A leech could cure a sick man but not a dying man, and an artillery piece could not hit targets beyond its range, whatever the state might wish. Craftsmen knew the limits of their art, but scientists dealt with matters of grander scope and fancied that their understanding was equal to the range of their imagination. The endorsement of teleology by Aristotle and Galen and the acceptance of astrology by Hipparchus and Ptolemy were sincere acts of personal faith but poor demonstrations of the scientific spirit of doubt and inquiry. The flame of science soon flickers when scientists embrace the occult.

Originally, Greek scientists worked independently but later succumbed to patronage and subsidies. Feeding on the state, Hellenistic scientists achieved brilliant feats in theory and practice, but the critical method was not applied to social or political problems, and many scientists were apologists for the existing order. Some scientists sought out the "corridors of power" and found them a dark labyrinth, which often housed strange monsters. In the Greco-Roman world, men of science were defenseless against persecution because the demands of society had priority over individual rights. There was more security for scientists at the Museum than in erratic Athens, but in both locales scholars were at the mercy of the state. Hellenistic scientists served "our mortal god," the state, but lacked the protection of sacerdotal status. Ironically, in the thirteenth century under an authoritarian church, Thomas Aquinas dismissed the cosmology of Genesis as the fable of an ignorant age,[131] and Dante advocated an Aristotelian planetary system which, like Copernicanism and Darwinism, contradicted scripture. Hellenistic scientists had been more cautious with dangerous ideas.

Although the phoenix is a pleasant myth, nothing is born from its own ashes. In the seventh century, the advanced centers of learning in the East fell into Muslim hands. Although the first impact of conquest was marred by occasional holocausts of pagan literature in Egypt and Iran, the servants of Allah succumbed to the sophistication of Syria and the life of science was preserved. Cut off from Alexandria and Antioch, Byzantine learning was soon desiccated. With great care, the scholars of Constantinople produced digests and encyclopedias which laid to rest the wisdom of the past. Meanwhile, Western Europe was an intellectual desert. Although Isidore of Seville was aware that the ancients had believed in the sphericity of the earth, scientific knowledge among the literate minority had sunk abjectly in the West. The few surviving Latin handbooks on science were poor digests and often depositories of misinformation.[132] Without adequate libraries and a knowledge of Greek, curiosity and common sense were insufficient to recapture the mastery of mind over nature. When Greek scientific works eventually returned to the West through the Muslims of Spain and Sicily, Medieval intellectuals quickly renewed the struggle to penetrate the secrets of nature, but the recovery of a high science was a slow process.

In the seventh century, the Byzantine state had come into possession of a secret incendiary weapon, Greek fire, which held Muslim armies at bay and was later used to repel Russian fleets. To awe visiting dignitaries from the backward West, the Byzantines employed the mechanical arts of ancient Greece. In the tenth century, Bishop Liudprand of Cremona visited Constantinople and complained that the Byzantines served oily food and wine mixed with "pitch, resin, and plaster." [133] However, Liudprand was impressed by the splendors of the palace:

Before the emperor's seat stood a tree, made of bronze gilded over, whose branches were filled with birds, also made of gilded bronze, which uttered different cries, each according to its varying species. The throne itself was so marvellously fashioned that at one moment it seemed a low structure, and at another it rose high into the air. It was of immense size and was guarded by lions, made either of bronze or of wood covered over with gold, who beat the ground with their tails and gave a dreadful roar with open mouth and quivering tongue. Leaning upon the shoulders of two eunuchs, I was brought into the emperor's presence. At my approach, the lions began to roar and the birds to cry out, each according to its kind; but I was neither terrified nor surprised, for I had previously made inquiry about all these things from people who were well acquainted with them. So after I had three times made obeisance to the emperor with my face upon the ground, I lifted my head, and behold! the man whom just before I had seen sitting on a moderately elevated seat had now changed his raiment and was sitting on the level of the ceiling. How it was done I could not imagine, unless perhaps he was lifted up by some such sort of device as we use for raising the timbers of a wine press.[134]

Employing the arts of Ctesibius and Archimedes to magnify the image of the state, the Byzantine rulers were true heirs of the Hellenistic kings who had used scientific tricks to awe the masses.

The failure of ancient society to fully exploit the ingenious machines of Ctesibius, Archimedes, and Hero has often been blamed on the widespread use of slaves. Throughout antiquity, the wealthy classes lived largely off rural rents or country estates operated by slaves. A few rich men employed slaves in industrial or service roles, and servile labor was both efficient and profitable, but these activities were peripheral to the overriding agrarian structure of ancient society. In this type of world, there was little incentive to invest capital in laborsaving technological improvements.[135] There was also another side to the problem of slavery and technology in antiquity. A. G. Drachmann correctly insists that

slave labor was not cheap, and the presence of slaves did not prevent the invention of the watermill, which could be constructed by the means in hand. The construction of the steam engine had to wait until it was possible to make iron pipes and put them together with screws.[136]

The distinguished historian Michael Rostovtzeff observed:

Ancient industry reached its highest level in the Hellenistic period when it was based solely on slave labor. It began to decay under the

Roman Empire when slaves were gradually replaced, even in the field of industry, by ever-increasing numbers of free workmen. . . . The weak point in the development of industry in the imperial period seems to have been the lack of real competition, and this lack depended entirely on the character, number, and buying capacity of the customers.[137]

Slave labor is quite practical in industry, and slaves were successfully employed in ironworks and textile factories in the American South before the Civil War.[138] However, slavery is economically harmful to the free population who do not own chattel. As the contracts of the Athenian Erechtheum and the records of the American South amply demonstrate, the wages of free workers are retarded by competition with skilled slave labor.[139] In antiquity, industrial production was confined to necessities for the many and luxuries for the few. Although every manufacturer tried to cut costs, new techniques and elaborate machines were not needed to produce cheap luxury articles for mass consumption. The ancient world lacked a mass market of consumers who could afford items other than food, clothing, and shelter.

From a technological viewpoint, the Greeks and Romans could have produced an industrial revolution by utilizing the knowledge of steam, air pressure, and meshing gears which was squandered on temple miracles and gadgets for the state. The recently recovered Antikythera computer dispels any doubt about ancient mechanical aptitude.[140] Although they did not use fossil fuels, the Greeks were aware of Near Eastern oil fields, where some deposits had accidentally ignited and burned for years.[141] Long before Eli Whitney, the Romans manufactured interchangeable parts for items to be assembled elsewhere.[142] An orientation toward mass consumption would surely have encouraged industrial research and the development of new techniques and better metals and fuels. However, the agrarian population was desperately poor, and wealth was concentrated in the cities: "The future of ancient industry depended on their purchasing power, and while the buying capacity of the city bourgeoisie was large, their numbers were limited, and the city proletariat grew steadily poorer." [143] The purchasing power of free men was too low to warrant mass production of nonnecessities, and thus science was not stimulated on a broad scale.[144] Since science cannot exist in a vacuum, the impetus for an industrial-scientific complex was prevented by the social and economic structure of ancient society. In the long run, poverty more than slavery sabotaged the mechanization of the ancient world.

Like the collapse of Athenian democracy and the failure of Roman militarism, the fate of science in antiquity should be a cause for reflection. The history of Greek science suggests that a scientific atmosphere may be as fragile as a soap bubble. Powerful and wealthy societies can support scientific research, but subsidies alone did not produce the great achievements of Greek science, which were accomplished by the genius of individuals. While Hellenistic kings invested in research for weapons and gadgets, the state was essentially indifferent to pure science. In any age, the search for truth is a matter of concern to only a few men. Despite the accomplishments of Hellenistic science, the status of the scientist in Greece and Rome was precarious. Alternately badgered, bought, tolerated, and dismissed, scientists were less secure than priests and were not always devoted to truth. In a sea of ignorance, the Museum stood as an isle of reason and scientific inquiry, but Hellenistic scientists cared little about the nature and dignity of man. Subsidized scientists did not wish to anger their patrons, the despotic rulers of Egypt and Rome, and, like those employers, the men of science were not immune to the contagion of irrationalism and occultism. Milton's lines on the blinded Samson might well apply to the scientists of the ancient world:

> Ask for this great Deliverer now, and find him
> Eyeless in Gaza at the Mill with slaves,
> Himself in bonds under Philistian yoke.

The analogy is not unjust, for future generations suffered because of the failure of science in Greece and Rome.

APPENDIX

A Historiographical Note

The historian of ancient science must face the general difficulty that besets all students of antiquity—the piecemeal nature of the sources. Ancient history is a mosaic in which episodes and figures have been preserved by chance, but the background is broken and the connecting pieces are often lost. Yet, for some events there is too much evidence—all of it contradictory. In general, the history of ideas in antiquity rests on a few texts and a great number of casual quotes. For the most part, the lives and careers of ancient scientists must be reconstructed from chance references and dubious anecdotes. Tales of martyrdom and clever retorts by sages to tyrants are commonplace, but even though they may have happened, such stories arouse critical suspicion. On the other hand, a sensible remark by a historian of the caliber of Polybius or Strabo may be quite plausible, but not necessarily true. The ultimate test of sources is inner consistency and corroboration by correlative material.

Obviously, eyewitness testimony deserves attention, but Strabo complained: "The same men went together and helped Alexander to conquer Asia, but these men often contradict each other. If they differ about what they saw, what can we believe of the things these men report from hearsay?" [1] Ancient writers of history often claimed objectivity, but they rarely attained it. Polybius, Josephus, and Tacitus loudly proclaimed their scholarly detachment and lack of bias, but their histories were riddled with value judgments and bitter partisan pleas. Impartiality is a modern ideal and should not be expected in the literature of the Greco-Roman world.

The means of literary transmission present additional problems. Most ancient works have perished or have been preserved in inept and careless epitomes. In the Augustan era, the mediocre compiler Diodorus Siculus copied freely from his betters and preserved valuable fragments of lost historians. In a characteristic passage, Diodorus referred to Ephorus of Cyme (fourth century B.C.) as "the most recent" authority on the Nile floods and proceeded to cite Agatharchides of Cnidus (second century B.C.) on the same subject—obviously Ephorus was recent to one of Diodorus' sources.[2] In the early second century A.D., Plutarch of Chaeronea often wrote from memory and always chose whatever version best suited the moral which he wished to draw from the events of history.[3] With customary carelessness, Plutarch confused the decree of Diopeithes with a number of similar episodes which were not related in time.[4] In another striking anachronism, he implied that Cimon's victory at the Eurymedon (467), the Peace of Callias (449?), and the Athenian Altar of Peace (374) were contemporary.[5] Historians of science who rely on Plutarch's statements would do well to compare the "facts" in his sketches of Themistocles and Aristides with the other sources which have survived. However, Plutarch was not a historian but a composer of moral essays and indifferent to the canons of scientific history.

In the third century A.D., Athenaeus of Naucratis composed the *Deipnosophistae* (or Gastronomers), a collection of quotations on many subjects, mostly culinary and often trivial. Although his bizarre book is a treasure house of lost authors, Athenaeus in one paragraph alone misquoted Strabo and confused the Stoic Posidonius with Panaetius.[6] A contemporary pedant, Diogenes Laertius, wrote an uncritical history of philosophy in biographical form which blurred many details and often attributed the same anecdotes to different famous men. Much of our information about early scientists and their ideas derive from such careless compilers as Diogenes Laertius, Aetius (second century A.D.?), and Stobaeus (fifth century A.D.). Theophrastus wrote a history of physics, Meno of medicine, and Eudemus of Rhodes of mathematics, but these works are lost and the history of ancient science will probably remain incomplete.

Regardless of reputation, no ancient author can be accepted on face value alone. Within the same historical setting, Plato referred to Pericles' death (429 B.C.) as recent, Archelaus as king of Macedon (not until 413), Nicias as still alive (before 413), and the trial of the Arginusae admirals as "last year" (405).[7] As a historian, Aristotle was careless and opinionated, and the celebrated history of the Athenian constitution, which he or his students composed, is a farrago of misinformation and doctrinaire distortions.[8] Even the greatest of Greek historians, Thucydides, could be brazenly wrong,[9] and Herodotus never rejected a good story whether it happened or not.[10] The fallibility of authority is not a problem confined to ancient history.

The foregoing remarks on authors and evidence should not be construed as a counsel of despair, but rather the statement of a problem. The history of antiquity has many gaps and some doubtful testimonies, but sufficient collateral evidence can be assembled to place most men and events within a useful frame of reference. Similarly, if the sources are used with caution, the history of ancient science can be reconstructed and may provide insights into a major aspect of the human past.

REFERENCE NOTES

INTRODUCTION: SCIENTISTS IN ANTIQUITY

1. See René Taton, *Reason and Chance in Scientific Discovery* (New York: Science Editions, 1962).
2. Otto Neugebauer, *The Exact Sciences in Antiquity* (Providence, R.I.: Brown University Press, Ed. 2, 1957), p. 208.
3. Giorgio de Santillana, *The Crime of Galileo* (Chicago: University of Chicago Press, 1955), p. ix.

CHAPTER ONE: THE GREEK WORLD

1. A. Seidenberg, "The Ritual Origin of Geometry," *Archive for History of Exact Sciences* (1962) 1:488–527. Hellenic tradition associated the duplication of a cube (the Delian problem) with doubling an altar— Plutarch, *de genio Socratis* 579BCD.
2. Seidenberg, *op. cit.*, p. 523.
3. Strabo XV 1.39. Because of the late composition of Indian historical records, the testimony of Greek visitors is of major significance, but see T. S. Brown, "The Reliability of Megasthenes," *American Journal of Philology* (1955) 76:18–33, and "The Merits and Weaknesses of Megasthenes," *Phoenix* (1957) 11:12–24.
4. Diodorus Siculus II 40.1–3. Strabo XV 1.39. Arrian, *Indica* 11. For a more reliable account of early Indic science, see David Pingree, "Astronomy and Astrology in India and Iran," *Isis* (1963) 54:229–246.
5. Diodorus Siculus II 41.5.
6. J. Eric S. Thompson, *The Rise and Fall of Maya Civilization* (Norman: University of Oklahoma Press, 1954), p. 87.
7. Wolfram Eberhard, "The Political Function of Astronomy and Astronomers in Han China," in *Chinese Thought and Institutions*, ed. John K. Fairbank (Chicago: University of Chicago Press, 1957), pp. 33–70.
8. *Ibid.*, p. 67.
9. Joseph Needham, *Science and Civilization in China* (Cambridge: Cambridge University Press, 1959), Vol. III, p. 193. For a later aspect of this problem, see George Wong, "China's Opposition to Western Science during the Late Ming and Early Ch'ing," *Isis* (1963) 54:29–49.
10. Liu Wu-Chi, *A Short History of Confucian Philosophy* (London: Penguin, 1955), p. 116. For another holocaust of historical books,

see George C. Vaillant, *The Aztecs of Mexico* (London: Penguin, 1951), p. 107.

11. Burton Watson, *Ssu-Ma Ch'ien, Grand Historian of China* (New York: Columbia University Press, 1958), pp. 66–67.
12. Strabo XVI 2.24. Cf. Diogenes Laertius IX 34.
13. Polybius XXXIV 2.7.
14. Herodotus II 109. Strabo XVII 1.3. Diodorus Siculus I 81.1–2.
15. Karl Marx, *Capital* (New York: Modern Library, no date), p. 564 n. 1.
16. Plutarch, *de Iside et Osiride* 365F. Diodorus Siculus I 27.4.
17. Henri Frankfort, ed., *The Intellectual Adventure of Ancient Man* (Chicago: University of Chicago Press, 1946), p. 80. See also John A. Wilson, *The Culture of Ancient Egypt* (Chicago: University of Chicago Press, 1956), p. 61.
18. Diodorus Siculus I 28.1; 73.5. However, Diodorus' sources are not unimpeachable. See T. W. Africa, "Herodotus and Diodorus on Egypt," *Journal of Near Eastern Studies* (1963) 22:254–258.
19. Karl A. Wittfogel, *Oriental Despotism* (New Haven: Yale University Press, 1957), pp. 29–30.
20. Adolf Erman, *The Literature of the Ancient Egyptians*, trans. Aylward M. Blackman (New York: Methuen & Company and Harper & Row, 1927), pp. 68–71.
21. Henry Sigerist, *A History of Medicine* (Oxford: Clarendon Press, 1951), Vol. I, pp. 298–359.
22. The standard study of Imhotep is Jamisson B. Hurry's *Imhotep the Vizier* (Oxford: Clarendon Press, 1928).
23. Homer, *Odyssey* IV 231.
24. Albert T. Olmstead, *History of the Persian Empire* (Chicago: University of Chicago Press, 1948), p. 143.
25. Martin Levey, "Some Objective Factors in Babylonian Medicine in the Light of New Evidence," *Bulletin of the History of Medicine* (1961) 35, 1:61–70. Sigerist, *op. cit.*, p. 410, is less favorable.
26. Code of Hammurabi 215–223, adapted from James Pritchard, ed., *Ancient Near Eastern Texts Relating to the Old Testament* (Princeton: Princeton University Press, Ed. 2, 1955), pp. 175–176.
27. Diodorus Siculus II 9.4.
28. Diodorus Siculus II 9.4; 29.2.
29. Diodorus Siculus II 30.5–31.9. Note the Hellenistic reference to Antigonus and Seleucus. The earliest personal horoscope dates from 410 B.C., see Neugebauer, *op. cit.*, p. 187.
30. Pliny, *Natural History* VII 193. Cicero, *de divinatione* I 36; cf. II 97.
31. Henry E. Sigerist; *op. cit.*, Vol. I, pp. 460–464.
32. Robert H. Pfeiffer, *State Letters of Assyria* (New Haven: American Oriental Society, 1935), No. 211, p. 154.
33. Isaiah 47.12–13.
34. Wisdom of Sirach 38.24–26; 39.1–4, trans. Edgar J. Goodspeed, *The*

Apocrypha (Chicago: University of Chicago Press, 1938), pp. 297–298.
35. Strabo XVI 2.24.
36. Diodorus Siculus I 96.2–3; 98.2–3. Ammianus Marcellinus XXII 16.19–22. Diogenes Laertius IX 34–35.
37. Strabo XVII 1.29–30.
38. Aristotle, *Metaphysics* I 1.981b.
39. Diodorus Siculus II 29.4–6. Posidonius is a likely source and may in turn rely on Berossus.
40. Homer, *Iliad* XI 514–515.
41. Homer, *Iliad* IV 217–219. Son of Asclepius: IV 193–194; II 731–733.
42. Cicero, *de natura deorum* III 39. The standard study on the god of medicine and his cult is Emma and Ludwig Edelstein, *Asclepius* (Baltimore: Johns Hopkins Press, 1945), 2 vols.
43. Diodorus Siculus V 74.6.
44. Cicero, *de natura deorum* III 57.
45. Strabo III 4.16. Diodorus Siculus V 26.3.
46. Strabo IV 4.5; VII 2.3. Diodorus Siculus V 29.4–5. Herodotus IV 64.
47. Diodorus Siculus IV 1.4–6. Cicero, *de natura deorum* I 38.
48. Polybius XXXIV 2.6.
49. Diodorus Siculus III 60.2–3.
50. Diodorus Siculus IV 27.5.
51. Strabo VII 3.9. Diogenes Laertius I 101.
52. Homer, *Iliad* XVIII 591–592.
53. Diodorus Siculus IV 76.1–3. Cf. Aristotle, *de anima* I 3.406b.
54. Diodorus Siculus IV 76.4–79.2. Cf. IV 30.1.
55. Michael Ventris and John Chadwick, *Documents in Mycenaean Greek* (Cambridge: Cambridge University Press, 1956), No. 200, pp. 306–307.
56. Hesiod, *Works and Days* 47–58; *Theogony* 521–570.
57. Aeschylus, *Prometheus Bound* 505–506.
58. Hesiod, *Theogony* 521–525. Athenaeus XV 672EF.
59. Pindar, *Pythia* I 96. Lucian, *Phalaris* I 11–12. Athenaeus IX 396E. To Aristotle (*Rhetoric* II 20.1393b), Phalaris was a conventional military tyrant.
60. Athenaeus XIII 602B.
61. Diodorus Siculus IX 19.
62. R. Hackforth, *The Cambridge Ancient History*, Vol. IV, p. 355. Polybius (XII 25.1–3) saw "Phalaris' bull" at Carthage, but T. S. Brown believes that the entire tale reflects Punic child sacrifice, *Timaeus of Tauromenium* (Berkeley: University of California Press, 1958), pp. 54–57.
63. Herodotus III 38.
64. Max Cary, *The Cambridge Ancient History*, Vol. III, p. 627.
65. Werner Jaeger, *Aristotle* (London: Oxford University Press, Ed.2, 1948), pp. 426–429.

104   Reference Notes

66. Plato, *Theaetetus* 174ABC, 175D. Diogenes Laertius IX 35–36. Aristotle, *Nicomachean Ethics* VI 7.1141b.
67. Diogenes Laertius IX 14.
68. Strabo XIV 1.16. Diogenes Laertius II 1–2, but see Herodotus II 109.
69. Herodotus III 60. The length of the tunnel was actually 1100 yards. See June Goodfield and Stephen Toulmin, "How Was the Tunnel of Eupalinus Aligned?" *Isis* (1965) 56:46–55. Compare Hezekiah's tunnel (II Kings 20.20; II Chronicles 32.30) and the Siloam Inscription, Pritchard, *op. cit.*, p. 321.
70. Herodotus IV 87–88; VII 36. See W. W. How and J. Wells, *A Commentary on Herodotus* (Cambridge: Cambridge University Press, 1912), Vol. II, pp. 142–144, for comments on Harpalus' bridge.
71. Herodotus I 74. Neugebauer, *op. cit.*, pp. 142–143, has refuted the legend of Thales' prediction of eclipses.
72. Diogenes Laertius I 22–23; 27.
73. Herodotus I 74–75.
74. Diogenes Laertius I 25.
75. Herodotus I 170. While the context suggests that Cyrus was the enemy, Miletus collaborated with the Persians.
76. Herodotus V 36. Cf. II 143.
77. Herodotus V 49–50.
78. Herodotus III 125, 129–137. Athenaeus XII 522BC.
79. Henry E. Sigerist, "On Hippocrates," *Bulletin of the History of Medicine* (1934) 2:190–214, is an excellent introduction to the topic of Hippocrates' life and probable works.
80. Plato, *Protagoras* 311B, *Phaedrus* 270C. Aristotle, *Politics* VII 4.1326a.
81. The definitive study of this famous document is by Ludwig Edelstein, "The Hippocratic Oath," *Bulletin of the History of Medicine*, Supplement I (Baltimore: 1943), pp. 1–64, esp. pp. 6–18, 38, 56–60.
82. Xenophon, *Anabasis* I 8.26–27. Plutarch, *Artaxerxes* 1, 11, 13, 18, 21. Cf. Diodorus Siculus II 32.4. For another Greek doctor who became a historian, see T. S. Brown, "Apollophanes and Polybius V," *Phoenix* (1961) 15:187–195.
83. Aristotle, *Metaphysics* XII 8.1073b.
84. Diogenes Laertius VIII 86–90. Diodorus Siculus I 98.4. Strabo XVII 1.29. Aristotle, *Nicomachean Ethics* X 1.1172b. Otto Neugebauer, *op. cit.*, p. 151, observes: "I see no good reason to deny the possibility of his travels to Egypt. It seems to me certain, however, that there was nothing to learn from the Egyptians themselves."
85. Diogenes Laertius V 1. The Greek, Latin, Syriac, and Arabic sources for the life of Aristotle are available in Ingemar Düring's "Aristotle in the Ancient Biographical Tradition," *Studia Graeca et Latina Gothoburgensia* (1957), Vol. V, pp. 13–476.
86. Diogenes Laertius V 3. Strabo XIII 1.57. Jaeger, *op. cit.*, pp. 112–117, doubts Hermias' connection with the Academy.
87. Plutarch, *Alexander* 8; 53–55; 77. Diogenes Laertius V 5.

88. Diogenes Laertius V 6.
89. Aristotle, Fragment 666 (Rose). Jaeger, *op. cit.*, p. 320, considers that "the tone of this fragment is very genuine."
90. Diogenes Laertius V 11.
91. Jaeger, *op. cit.*, p. 337.
92. Aristotle, *Parts of Animals* I 5.645a, trans. William Ogle, *The Works of Aristotle* (Oxford: Clarendon Press, 1912), Vol. V, p. 644.
93. Charles Darwin, *The Origin of Species* (New York: Modern Library, no date), pp. 373–374.
94. Thucydides I 3, but cf. Homer, *Iliad* II 867, and Strabo XIV 2.28.
95. Herodotus IX 62.
96. Sophocles, *Ajax* 1288–1292, trans. R. C. Trevelyan in *The Complete Greek Drama* (New York: Random House, 1938), Vol. I, pp. 355–356.
97. Thucydides I 6.
98. Plato, *Protagoras* 337C.
99. Oxyrhynchus Papyrus 1364 (Diels⁵ fragment B44). Cf. William Shakespeare, *Merchant of Venice*, III i 54–62.
100. *Airs, Waters, and Places* 16. Cf. 24.
101. Euripides, *Iphigenia in Aulis* 1400–1401. Aristotle approved, *Politics* I 2.1252b.
102. Xenophon, *Hellenica* III 4.19. Athenaeus XII 550E. Plutarch, *Agesilaus* 9.
103. Plato, *Republic* IV 435E–436A, V 470A.
104. Isocrates, *Panegyricus* 50; *Address to Philip* 154.
105. Aristotle, *Politics* VII 7.1327b, trans. Ernest Barker (New York: Oxford University Press, 1958), p. 296. Cf. I 8.1256b on the natural justice of colonial wars. The *Politics* postdates the murder of Philip (V 10.1311b) whose policy of imperialism was enthusiastically continued by Alexander. Ernst Badian, "Alexander the Great and the Unity of Mankind," *Historia* (1958) 7:440–444, believes that VII 7.1327b represents a mellowing of Aristotle's views on barbarians as contrasted with earlier passages (e.g. I 2.1252b) in the *Politics* and the extremely harsh statement that they should be treated as "plants and animals" (see footnote 108, below). However, the relative dating of the composition of different parts of the *Politics* is a much disputed topic, and we simply do not know when Aristotle wrote his callous advice about barbarians as "plants and animals."
106. Plutarch, *Camillus* 22.
107. Aristotle, *Politics* II 11.1272b.
108. Plutarch, *de Alexandri magni fortuna aut virtute* 329B.
109. Diogenes Laertius VIII 60–61; 70.
110. Diogenes Laertius VIII 51; 63; 66.
111. Aristotle, *de respiratione* 7.473b. Cf. *Physics* IV 6.213a. However, see D. J. Furley, "Empedocles and the Clepsydra," *Journal of Hellenic Studies* (1957) 77:31–34, and N. B. Booth, "Empedocles' Account of Breathing," *Journal of Hellenic Studies* (1960) 80:10–15.

112. Strabo XIV 1.16. Diogenes Laertius VIII 3.
113. Diodorus Siculus X 3.2. Justin XX 4. Porphyry, *Life of Pythagoras* 18. A standard monograph is Kurt von Fritz's *Pythagorean Politics in Southern Italy* (New York: Columbia University Press, 1940).
114. Porphyry, *Life of Pythagoras* 19. Diogenes Laertius VIII 4–5. Diodorus Siculus X 3.5; 5.1–10.2.
115. Bertrand Russell, *A History of Western Philosophy* (New York: Simon and Schuster, 1945), p. 31.
116. Diodorus Siculus X 4.1–6; 8.1–3. Cicero, *de officiis* III 45; *Tusculan Disputations* V 63.
117. Diogenes Laertius VIII 3. Diodorus Siculus XII 9.2–10. Porphyry, *Life of Pythagoras* 21–22.
118. Aristotle in Diogenes Laertius VIII 34, but see VIII 24 and Porphyry, *Life of Pythagoras* 44.
119. Diodorus Siculus XII 20.1–21.3. Strabo VI 1.8. Cf. Athenaeus X 429A. The Sicilian historian Timaeus doubted that Zaleucus ever existed—Cicero, *de legibus* II 15.
120. Diodorus Siculus XII 17.1–5.
121. Aristotle, *Politics* II 12.1274ab. Cf. Diodorus Siculus XII 11.1–19.2.
122. Diodorus Siculus XII 12.4. See the comment of Henri I. Marrou, *A History of Education in Antiquity* (New York: Mentor, 1964), pp. 159–160.
123. Diodorus Siculus XII 13.4.
124. Louis Cohn-Haft, "The Public Physicians of Ancient Greece," *Smith College Studies in History* (1956) Vol. XLII, p. 54.
125. Strabo VI 1.12.
126. G. S. Kirk and J. E. Raven, *The Presocratic Philosophers* (Cambridge: Cambridge University Press, 1957), p. 233. See also the discussion of Alcmaeon by Henry Sigerist, *History of Medicine*, Vol. II, pp. 101–104.
127. Diogenes Laertius VIII 83. Aristotle, *Metaphysics* I 5.986a.
128. Aetius V 30.1.
129. Appian, *Mithridatic War* 28, felt that the Pythagoreans were worse than conventional despots and deserved comparison with Critias and the Thirty at Athens.
130. Diodorus Siculus X 11.1–2. Diogenes Laertius VIII 39–40. Plutarch, *de genio Socratis* 583A.
131. Polybius II 39.1–7. Strabo VIII 7.1.
132. Aristotle, *de caelo* II 13.293ab. Aetius II 7.7. See Sir Thomas Heath, *Aristarchus of Samos* (Oxford: Clarendon Press, 1913), pp. 94–119, and Walter Burkert, *Weisheit und Wissenschaft* (Nürnberg: Hans Carl, 1962), pp. 203–277, 315–335.
133. Diogenes Laertius VIII 85. Aulus Gellius III 17.1–6.
134. Diogenes Laertius VIII 84 refers to Philolaus but probably meant Dion.

135. Diogenes Laertius VIII 79. Strabo VI 3.4.
136. Diogenes Laertius VIII 82–83. Aulus Gellius X 12.9–10. Aristotle, *Politics* VIII 6.1340b.
137. Plato, *Epistle* IX 357e–358b, trans. Glenn R. Morrow, *Plato's Epistles* (New York: Bobbs Merrill, 1962), pp. 258–259.
138. Representative critics of Plato are Warner Fite, *The Platonic Legend* (New York: Scribners, 1934), Hans Kelsen, "Platonic Love," *American Imago* (1942) 3:3–110, and K. R. Popper, *The Open Society and Its Enemies* (Princeton: Princeton University Press, Ed. 2, 1950). Ronald B. Levinson, *In Defense of Plato* (Cambridge, Mass.: Harvard University Press, 1953) defends Plato against his critics.
139. Plutarch, *Dion* 5. Diogenes Laertius III 19–20.
140. Plato, *Epistle* VII *passim*. Diogenes Laertius III 3. On the mercenary traits of Plato and other philosophers, see Philostratus, *Life of Apollonius* I 34.
141. Plutarch, *Dion* 28. Athenaeus XI 508EF. Cf. Memnon's account of the "Platonic" tyrant Clearchus, in Jacoby *F.Gr.H.* 434 F 1.
142. Plutarch, *adversus Colotem* 1126A, lists a number of famous graduates of the Academy.
143. Athenaeus XI 508F. Diogenes Laertius III 46.
144. Plutarch, *Philopoemen* 1; *Aratus* 5. Cf. the murder of Cotys of Thrace by Academics—Philostratus, *Life of Apollonius* VII 2.
145. Diogenes Laertius IX 40. Plato, *Laws* XII 967BC.
146. Plato, *Republic* II 377D–378F.
147. Plato, *Laws* XII 967BC; VII 821B–822C.
148. Plato, *Laws* X 907D–909F.
149. E. R. Dodds, *The Greeks and the Irrational* (Berkeley: University of California Press, 1951), p. 224.
150. Aristotle, *Politics* III 11.1282a, includes a third category of educated laymen with a general knowledge of medicine. See also Owsei Temkin, "Greek Medicine as Science and Craft," *Isis* (1953) 44:213–222.
151. Plato, *Laws* IV 720A–D, IX 857CD.
152. Polybius XII 25d.
153. Herodotus II 167. M. I. Finley, "Was Greek Civilization Based on Slave Labor," *Historia* (1959) 8:154–155, comments perceptively on the general bias against the dignity of labor: "Throughout the centuries, no ideology of labor appeared, nothing that can in any sense be counterposed to the negative judgments with which the writings of the leisure class are filled. There was neither a word in the Greek language with which to express the general notion of 'labor,' nor the concept of labor 'as a general social function.'"
154. Aristotle, *Politics* I 11.1258b.
155. Aristotle, *Politics* III 4.1277a–1278a.
156. Xenophon, *Oeconomicus* IV 2–3.
156a. M. I. Finley, *op. cit.*, p. 154, observes: "It is a commonplace that the little man shares the ideals and aspirations of his betters—in his

dreams if not in the hard reality of his daily life. By and large, the vast majority in all periods of history have always taken the basic institutions of society for granted."

157. Xenophon, *Memorabilia* II 8.1–5.
158. Bertrand Gille in *A History of Technology*, ed. Singer, Holmyard, Hall, and Williams (Oxford: Clarendon Press, 1957), Vol. II, p. 638. See also Derek J. de Solla Price, *Science Since Babylon* (New Haven: Yale University Press, 1961), p. 42.
159. Plutarch, *Marcellus* 17. Giorgio de Santillana, *The Origins of Scientific Thought* (Chicago: University of Chicago Press, 1961), p. 239, believes that this passage does not reflect Archimedes' views but only Plutarch's "pious Platonism."
160. Aristotle, Fragment 52 (Rose), trans. Jaeger, *op. cit.*, p. 91.
161. Plato, *Republic* VII 529A–530A.
162. T. W. Africa, "Copernicus' Relation to Aristarchus and Pythagoras," *Isis* (1961) 52:403–409. See also Edward Rosen, "Was Copernicus a Pythagorean," *Isis* (1962) 53:504–508, and the reply, p. 509.
163. Aristotle, *Physics* IV 2.209b.
164. Plato, *Epistle* VII 341e, trans. Morrow, p. 238. George Grote, Eduard Meyer, and most historians accept the seventh epistle as authentic, but some scholars deny that Plato wrote it. A recent attack on the authenticity of the epistle is by Ludwig Edelstein, "Plato's Seventh Letter," *Philosophia Antiqua* (1966) XIV: 1–171.
165. Thucydides II 41.
166. Diogenes Laertius II 7. Anaxagoras was older than Empedocles— Aristotle, *Metaphysics* I 3.984a.
167. Plutarch, *Pericles* 4–5; 16.
168. Plutarch, *Pericles* 35. Cicero, *de republica* I 25. Thucydides II 28; VII 50.
169. Diogenes Laertius II 7.
170. Diogenes Laertius II 12. Diodorus Siculus XII 39.2 dates these events in 431 B.C., but see Sir Frank Adcock, *The Cambridge Ancient History*, Vol. V, pp. 477–478, and A. E. Taylor, "The Date of the Trial of Anaxagoras," *Classical Quarterly* (1917) 11:81–87.
171. Diogenes Laertius II 14–15. Aristotle, *Rhetoric* II 23.1398b.
172. Diodorus Siculus XII 36.2.
173. The Athenian calendar is a controversial and complicated subject. See B. L. van der Waerden, "Greek Astronomical Calendars and their Relation to the Athenian Civil Year," *Journal of Hellenic Studies* (1960) 80:168–180.
174. Scholiast, Aristophanes *Birds* 997 (Philochorus, Jacoby 328 F 122).
175. Plutarch, *Nicias* 13.
176. Aristophanes, *Birds* 995–1015, trans. R. H. Webb, in *The Complete Plays of Aristophanes*, ed. Moses Hadas (New York: Bantam Books, 1962), pp. 264–265. Reprinted by permission of Mrs. R. H. Webb and the University Press of Virginia.

177. Werner Jaeger, *Paideia* (New York: Oxford University Press, Ed. 2, 1945), Vol. I, p. 340.
178. Thucydides II 47–54. The literature on the plague is enormous. Three recent suggestions on the nature of the pestilence are (measles) D. L. Page, "Thucydides' Description of the Great Plague at Athens," *Classical Quarterly* (1953) N.S. 3:97–119; (typhus) W. Mac-Arthur, "The Athenian Plague: A Medical Note," *Classical Quarterly* (1954) N.S. 4: 171–174; and (glanders) Clifford Eby and Harold Evjen, "The Plague at Athens: A New Oar in Muddied Waters," *Journal of the History of Medicine* (1962) 17:258–263.
179. Plutarch, *Pericles* 32.
180. W. R. Connor, "Two Notes on Diopeithes the Seer," *Classical Philology* (1963) 58:115–118.
181. *Ibid.*, p. 116. Thucydides VIII 1.
182. Xenophon, *Hellenica* III 3.3. Plutarch, *Lysander* 22, *Agesilaus* 3.
183. J. B. Bury, *The Cambridge Ancient History*, Vol. V, p. 383.
184. Diogenes Laertius IX 50. See Victor Ehrenberg, "The Foundations of Thurii," *American Journal of Philology* (1948) 59:168–169.
185. Diogenes Laertius IX 51.
186. Plutarch, *Pericles* 26. Diogenes Laertius IX 24.
187. Diogenes Laertius IX 54. Cf. Aristotle, *Constitution of Athens* 29.1–2, and Xenophon, *Hellenica* II 3.1.
188. Plato, *Meno* 91DEF.
189. Dodds, *op. cit.*, p. 201, n. 66.
190. W. S. Ferguson, *The Cambridge Ancient History*, Vol. V, p. 279. The pursuit of Protagoras by Athenian cruisers is a late romantic touch— Philostratus, *Lives of the Sophists* I 10.494.
191. Diogenes Laertius IX 52. Cicero, *de natura deorum* I 63.
192. Thucydides VI 60.
193. Diodorus Siculus XIII 6.7. Athenaeus XIII 611B. Aristophanes, *Birds* 1072–1073.
194. Lysias, *against Andocides* 17. Cicero, *de natura deorum* I 2; 63. Diogenes Laertius VI 59. Leonard Woodbury, "The Date and Atheism of Diagoras of Melos," *Phoenix* (1965) 19:178–211, doubts that Diagoras was a thoroughgoing atheist.
195. Plutarch, *Nicias* 23, trans. Ian Scott-Kilvert, *The Rise and Fall of Athens* (London: Penguin, 1960), pp. 236–237.
196. Plato, *Apology* 26D.
197. Victor Ehrenberg, *The People of Aristophanes* (New York: Schocken Books, Ed. 3, 1962), p. 280.
198. Plato, *Phaedo* 97B–98C.
199. Xenophon, *Memorabilia* IV 7.2–10.
200. Cicero, *Tusculan Disputations* V 104. Diogenes Laertius IX 36.
201. Aristotle, Fragment 668 (Rose). See Jaeger, *Aristotle*, pp. 321–322.
202. Diogenes Laertius II 101.
203. Polybius XII 13.11.

204. Diogenes Laertius V 38.
205. Athenaeus XIII 610EF.

CHAPTER TWO: THE HELLENISTIC WORLD
1. Plato, *Epistle* II 310e, trans. Morrow, p. 194.
2. Vitruvius VI preface 2.
3. Diogenes Laertius V 37.
4. Diogenes Laertius V 38; 51; 53.
5. Diogenes Laertius V 58.
6. Cicero, *Academica* I 34.
7. Polybius III 59.3–5.
8. Ammianus Marcellinus XV 1.4. Anaxarchus also relieved Alexander's fear of astrological predictions, Diodorus Siculus XVII 112.4–5 and Justin XII 13.
9. Plutarch, *Alexander* 8; 28; 52. Diogenes Laertius IX 60.
10. Diogenes Laertius IX 63.
11. Diogenes Laertius IX 58–59.
12. Diogenes Laertius II 115.
13. Diogenes Laertius V 77–78.
14. Diogenes Laertius II 102.
15. Diogenes Laertius II 103. Athenaeus XII 611B. Cicero, *Tusculan Disputations* I 102.
16. Athenaeus IV 162EF.
17. Diogenes Laertius VII 9; 36. Athenaeus IV 162BCD; XIII 607A–F. Plutarch, *Aratus* 18; 23.
18. Diogenes Laertius VII 177; 185. Plutarch, *Cleomenes* 11.
19. Diogenes Laertius II 110.
20. Diogenes Laertius IV 38–39; V 67.
21. Cicero, *de republica* I 34. Velleius Paterculus I 13.3. Plutarch, *Pompey* 42.
22. Athenaeus VI 253CDE.
23. Diodorus Siculus V 46.2–7; VI 1.1–10. See T. S. Brown, "Euhemerus and the Historians," *Harvard Theological Review* (1946) 39:265–266.
24. Diodorus Siculus I 15.4.
25. Diodorus Siculus IV 71.4.
26. Vitruvius II preface 1–3. Strabo XIV 1.23.
27. Vitruvius II preface 4.
28. Diodorus Siculus I 34.2. Vitruvius X 6.1–4. Strabo XVII 1.52.
29. Diodorus Siculus V 37.3–4.
30. Plutarch, *Marcellus* 14. Vitruvius IX preface 9–12.
31. Two authoritative surveys of Ptolemaic Egypt are Michael Rostovtzeff's *The Social and Economic History of the Hellenistic World* (Oxford: Clarendon Press, 1941), Vol. I, pp. 255–422, and W. W. Tarn's *Hellenistic Civilization* (London: E. Arnold, Ed. 3, 1952), pp. 177–209.
32. W. W. Tarn, *op. cit.*, p. 198.
33. Based on Arthur S. Hunt and J. G. Smyly, *The Tebtunis Papyri*

(London: Oxford University Press, 1933), Vol. III–1, No. 703, lines 222–234.

34. A standard discussion of the Museum is the article, "Museion," by Müller-Graupa in Pauly-Wissowa-Kroll, *Real-Encyclopädie der classischen Altertumswissenschaft*, Vol. XXXI, cols. 801–820.

35. Theocritus XIV 59.

36. Athenaeus I 22D, trans. Sir John E. Sandys, *A History of Classical Scholarship* (Cambridge: Cambridge University Press, Ed. 2, 1906), Vol. I, p. 103.

37. Strabo XVII 1.8. Cf. Vitruvius V 11.2.

38. Michael Rostovtzeff, *op. cit.*, Vol. II, p. 1084.

39. Otto Neugebauer, *American Journal of Philology* (1964) 85:420, sounds a caustic cautionary note against romanticising scientific activity at Alexandria.

40. Plutarch, *Demetrius* 38. Tarn, *op. cit.*, pp. 305–306, rejects this passage as apocryphal.

41. Strabo I 4.9.

42. Vitruvius IX 8.2–7. Pliny, *Natural History* VII 125. Athenaeus XI 497DE; IV 174BDE. For the date of Ctesibius, see A. G. Drachmann, "Ktesibios, Philon, and Heron: A Study in Ancient Pneumatics," *Acta Historica Scientiarum Naturalium et Medicanalium* (1948) 4:1–3, and "On the Alleged Second Ctesibius," *Centaurus* (1951) 2:1–10.

43. A. G. Drachmann, "Ktesibios," p. 140.

44. Michael Rostovtzeff, *op. cit.*, Vol. II, pp. 1090–1093.

45. Celsus, *de medicina*, preface 23–24.

46. Celsus, *de medicina*, preface 40–43, 74. Ludwig Edelstein accepts the charge as true, "The Development of Greek Anatomy," *Bulletin of the History of Medicine* (1935) 3:235–248, esp. pp. 238, 246.

47. Miguel de Asin, "The Pharos of Alexandria," *Proceedings of the British Academy* (1933) 19:277–292.

48. Athenaeus V 203CE.

49. Athenaeus V 203E–206C.

50. Athenaeus V 206D–209E. Cf. Plutarch, *Marcellus* 14.

51. Strabo XVII 1.5. Diodorus Siculus III 36.3–37.8.

52. Tarn, *Hellenistic Civilisation*, p. 307. The bear may have been an albino Syrian bear, Athenaeus V 201C.

53. Diodorus Siculus III 18.4; 42.1.

54. Herodotus IV 42.

55. Strabo II 3.4.

56. Strabo II 3.4–5. Strabo does not believe a word of the story.

57. Rostovtzeff, *op. cit.*, Vol. II, pp. 926–928, and Tarn, *Hellenistic Civilisation*, pp. 247–249.

58. Strabo I 2.26.

59. The Carthaginians reached Sierra Leone. See Max Cary and E. H. Warmington, *The Ancient Explorers* (New York: Penguin, 1963), pp. 63–68.

60. Pliny, *Natural History* VI 58.

61. Strabo II 5.12. Pliny, *Natural History* VI 101–106. See Rostovtzeff, *op. cit.*, Vol. II, p. 929.
62. Athenaeus XIV 652E–653A.
63. N. A. Kiman and R. McKeon, *The Edicts of Asoka* (Chicago: University of Chicago Press, 1959), Rock Edict XIII, p. 29.
64. Acts of the Apostles XVII 16–32.
65. Strabo XV 1.73. Dio Cassius LIV 9.8–10. Cf. *Res Gestae Divi Augusti* 31. Rudolf Bultmann, *The History of the Synoptic Tradition* (New York: Harper & Row, 1963), p. 292, believes that the story of the Magi had its origin in the Arabian cult of Dusares.
66. Strabo I 2.1, also credits the Parthians with revealing Central Asia and Mithridates of Pontus with exposing Colchis and the Sea of Azov.
67. Strabo XIII 4.2.
68. The Letter of Aristeas 10. Aulus Gellius VII 17.3. Although there were two state libraries in the city, the term "Alexandrian Library" usually includes the total collections of books at Alexandria.
69. Plutarch, *Antony* 58. Although Ammianus Marcellinus (XXII 16.13) claims that 700,000 books perished, Seneca relies on Livy and says that only 40,000 books were burned, *de animi tranquillitate* 9.5.
70. Plutarch, *Aemilius Paullus* 28.
71. Strabo XIII 1.54. Plutarch, *Sulla* 26. Athenaeus I 3AB. Felix Grayeff, "The Problem of the Genesis of Aristotle's Text," *Phronesis* (1956) 1:105–122, doubts the story of the loss of the texts but insists that the *Corpus Aristotelicum* is in fact a *Corpus Peripateticum* (pp. 109, 118–119).
72. Diogenes Laertius VII 186.
73. Cicero, *Tusculan Disputations* I 83.
74. Vitruvius VII preface 8–9. While the date and identity of Zoilus are disputed, his relation to his royal patron is consistent with the era. See Sandys, *op. cit.*, Vol. I, pp. 108–110.
75. Athenaeus IV 184BC. For a more favorable view of Ptolemy VII, see Tarn, *Hellenistic Civilisation*, pp. 205–206, and Rostovtzeff, *op. cit.*, Vol. II, pp. 878–895.
76. Edward A. Parsons, *The Alexandrian Library* (Amsterdam: The American Elsevier Press, 1952), p. 152.
77. Suetonius, *Claudius* 42.
78. Naphtali Lewis, "The Non-Scholars of the Alexandrian Museum," *Mnemosyne* (1963) Ser. 4, Vol. 16:257–261.
79. Athenaeus VI 240B; XV 677E. Philostratus, *Lives of the Sophists* I 22.524.
80. Plutarch, *Pericles* 27. Diodorus Siculus XII 28.2–3.
81. Vitruvius X 13.4–8. Arrian, *Alexander* II 18–24. Diodorus Siculus XVII 41.1–46.4.
82. Strabo XIV 2.5.
83. Plutarch, *Demetrius* 21–22. Diodorus Siculus XX 92.1–95.5.
84. Diodorus Siculus XX 96.1–3; 98.1.
85. Vitruvius X 16.3–6. Diodorus Siculus XX 91.2–8.

86. Diodorus Siculus XX 48.1–8.
87. Diodorus Siculus XX 96.3–97.7.
88. Vitruvius X 16.7–8. Vitruvius (16.5) notes the diminishing returns in excessive size of machinery.
89. Diodorus Siculus XX 99.1–100.4.
90. H. Marton, "The Colossus of Rhodes," *Journal of Hellenic Studies* (1956) 76:68–86.
91. Herodotus IV 200. cf. V 115; VI 18.
92. Vitruvius X 16.9–10.
93. Polybius XXI 27.1–28.17.
94. An excellent illustrated survey of Greek and Roman military technology may be found in the section by A. R. Hall in *A History of Technology*, ed. Singer et al., Vol. II, pp. 695–730.
95. Aeneas Tacticus I 3, 6–7; III 3; V 1; X 3–7, 11, 15, 20, 26; XI 1; XII 2; XIV 1–2; XVII 1.
96. Aeneas Tacticus, Fragment 4 (London: Loeb Classics, 1923).
97. Rostovtzeff, *op. cit.*, Vol. II, p. 1083. The reference to Athenaeus is to the Augustan writer, Athenaeus the Mechanic, and not to the author of the *Deipnosophistae*.
98. Cicero, *de oratore* II 75–76.
99. Philo of Byzantium, *Mechanics* IV 3.5, trans. Morris Cohen and I. E. Drabkin, *A Source Book in Greek Science* (Cambridge, Mass: Harvard University Press, 1958), p. 318.
100. A. G. Drachmann, *The Mechanical Technology of Greek and Roman Antiquity* (Madison: University of Wisconsin Press, 1963), pp. 189–190.
101. Plutarch, *Marcellus* 15–17. Polybius VIII 3.1–7.9. Livy XXIV 34.
102. Galen, *de temperamentis* III 2, in the second century A.D. is the earliest source for this tale; his contemporary, Lucian, *Hippias* 2, refers only to burning ships and does not mention mirrors. According to Zonaras, Dio Cassius XV 9.4 recounted the story of the mirrors in the early third century. A similar legend grew out of the use of a prototype of Greek fire at Constantinople in 514 A.D.—see J. B. Bury, *History of the Later Roman Empire* (New York: Dover, 1958) Vol. I, pp. 451–452. W. E. Knowles Middleton, "Archimedes, Kircher, Buffon, and the Burning Mirrors," *Isis* (1961) 52:533–543, argues that the tale of the burning mirrors is plausible: "Buffon did it, and it is reasonable to assume that Archimedes could have done it too, whether he did it or not." (p. 543) However, Knowles Middleton seems unaware of the historiographic complexity of the tradition, for he cites Gibbon (Bury ed., Vol. IV, pp. 242–243) as authoritative. It is significant that neither Polybius, Livy, nor Plutarch mentions the mirrors, although they described Archimedes' weapons in detail. Polybius was a professional historian of the second century B.C. and consulted eyewitness accounts of the siege of Syracuse. Livy, in the first century B.C., was also a trained historian and used Polybius' works as well as Roman annalists. It is inconceivable that Plutarch, who

recounted Archimedes' war machines with great relish, would have overlooked such a feat as the burning mirrors. Futhermore, if there had been such devices in Syracuse, the Romans would have seized them intact and utilized them in future wars. Apparently, some antique Münchhausen, not Archimedes, invented the remarkable mirrors.

103. Livy XXV 31. Pliny, *Natural History* VII 125. Plutarch, *Marcellus* 19, says that Archimedes was killed while resisting arrest. Cf. Dio Cassius XV 9.5.

104. Edward MacCurdy ed., *The Notebooks of Leonardo da Vinci* (New York: Garden City, 1941), p. 850.

105. Sir Frank E. Adcock, *The Greek and Macedonian Art of War* (Berkeley: University of California Press, 1957), pp. 62–63.

106. Herodian III 9.5.

107. Strabo XV 1.34.

108. Donald R. Dudley, *A History of Cynicism* (London: Methuen, 1937), pp. 91–92. Cf. Diogenes Laertius VI 28.

109. Rostovtzeff, *op. cit.*, Vol. II, pp. 1130–1132. The opportunistic career of Sphaerus does not affect the general conservatism of the Stoics. See T. W. Africa, *Phylarchus and the Spartan Revolution* (Berkeley: University of California Press, 1961), pp. 16–18, and H. C. Baldry, "Zeno's Ideal State," *Journal of Hellenic Studies* (1959) 73:3–15.

110. Diogenes Laertius II 143.

111. Strabo XIV 5.14.

112. Diogenes Laertius X 25.

113. Diogenes Laertius X 119.

114. Plutarch, *Sulla* 12. Pausanias I 20.5–6. Strabo IX 1.20. Athenaeus V 211D–215B. Posidonius calls him Athenion after his father, a Peripatetic.

115. Appian, *Mithridatic War* 28. Athenaeus V 215BC calls the tyrant Lysias of Tarsus an Epicurean, but Athenaeus also labeled Aristion a Peripatetic.

116. Benjamin Farrington has argued this thesis in *Science and Politics in the Ancient World* (New York: Oxford University Press, 1940), *Head and Hand in Ancient Greece* (London: Watts, 1947), and *Greek Science* (London: Penguin, 1953). See Arnaldo Momigliano's review of *Science and Politics* in *Journal of Roman Studies* (1941) 31:149–157.

117. Athenaeus XIII 547A. A purge of philosophers by "King Antiochus" (547B) is doubtful.

118. Lucian, *Alexander the False Prophet* 25; 47.

119. Cicero, *epistulae ad familiares* XV 16.1–3. Plutarch, *Brutus* 37. Cf. William Shakespeare, *Julius Caesar* V i 79–81.

120. Lily R. Taylor, *Party Politics in the Age of Caesar* (Berkeley: University of California Press, 1949), pp. 28–29, 96.

121. Diogenes Laertius X 85–87, transl. R. D. Hicks (London: Loeb Classics, 1931), Vol. II, p. 615.

122. Diodorus Siculus III 66.2. Pliny, *Natural History* II 231. Pausanias VI 26.1–2. See Campbell Bonner, "A Dionysiac Miracle at Corinth," *American Journal of Philology* (1929) 33:368–375.
123. Drachmann, "Ktesibios," p. 127.
124. Claudian XLVIII, M. Platnauer ed. (London: Loeb Classics, 1922), Vol. II, pp. 235–239. See Farrington's comment, *Greek Science*, p. 200 n. 1.
125. Plutarch, *Cleomenes* 39. See Eugene McCartney, "Spontaneous Generation and Kindred Notions in Antiquity," *Transactions of the American Philological Association* (1920) 51:106–107.
126. Alexis, Fragment 30, trans. T. F. Higham, *The Oxford Book of Greek Verse in Translation* (Oxford: Clarendon Press, 1953), p. 524.
127. Marrou, *op. cit.*, pp. 253–255.
128. Neugebauer, *op. cit.*, pp. 168–171, 187–189.
129. Martin Nilsson, "Origin of the Belief in the Divinity of Heavenly Bodies," *Harvard Theological Review* (1940) 33:1–8.
130. Aristotle, *Metaphysics* XII 8.1074b.
131. Cicero, *de divinatione* II 87–88.
132. Cicero, *de divinatione* I 93–94.
133. Cicero, *de divinatione* I 5. Cf. Diogenes Laertius X 135.
134. Diogenes Laertius VII 149. Cicero, *de divinatione* I 10.
135. Cicero, *de divinatione* I 6.
136. Diogenes Laertius VII 174.
137. Diogenes Laertius VII 170.
138. Plutarch, *de facie quae in orbe lunae apparet* 923A. The Hearth was the earth, Hestia, who stays at home while the Twelve Great Gods parade through the Zodiac—Plato, *Phaedrus* 247A. To Cleanthes, the Sun was the "leader of the cosmos"—Diogenes Laertius VII 139.
139. Pierre Duhem, *Le Système du Monde* (Paris: A. Hermann, 1913), Vol. I, p. 423. Ernst Zinner, *Die Geschichte der Sternkunde* (Berlin: J. Springer, 1931), p. 100. Gilbert Murray, *Five Stages of Greek Religion* (New York: Beacon, 1951), p. 141. E. R. Dodds, *op. cit.*, p. 246. Farrington, *Greek Science*, p. 228, even insists that "the stability of ancient oligarchical society" was connected with geocentrism.
139a. Most scholars assume that Aristarchus gravitated to the Museum, but George Sarton, *A History of Science* (Cambridge, Mass.: Harvard University Press, 1959), Vol. II, p. 54, doubts that he was at Alexandria. Yet, Aristarchus could have studied with Strato in Egypt before 286 b.c. On the other hand, Samos was Ptolemaic territory after 280, and Aristarchus would naturally seek the patronage of his sovereign.
140. E. J. Dijksterhuis, *The Arenarius of Archimedes* (Leiden: Brill, 1956), pp. 20–21.
141. J. L. Dreyer, *A History of Astronomy from Thales to Kepler* (New York: Dover, Ed. 2, 1953), p. 148. Sir Thomas Heath, *op. cit.*, p. 308. Cf. Edwin A. Burtt, *The Metaphysical Foundations of Modern Physical Science* (London: Routledge and Kegan, 1951), p. 25.

142. Seleucus was interested in ocean tides and accepted diurnal rotation to explain the phenomenon—Hermann Diels, *Doxographi Graeci* (Berlin: W. de Gruyter, 1929), p. 383. Cf. Strabo I 1.9; XVI 1.6. Plutarch, *platonicae quaestiones* VIII 1006C, says the Seleucus accepted Aristarchus' hypothesis of the earth "turning and revolving" as true, but it is not clear that anything more than diurnal rotation was meant, for Plutarch then refers to Plato's adherence in his old age to the Pythagorean system of Philolaus (cf. *Numa* 11) and cites Theophrastus as the source of this information, which has nothing to do with the beliefs of Aristarchus. Sir Thomas Heath, *op. cit.*, pp. 305–307, and most scholars feel that Seleucus endorsed the heliocentric hypothesis, but J. L. Dreyer, *op. cit.*, p. 140 n. 2 and p. 82, believes that Seleucus accepted only diurnal rotation.

143. Sir Thomas Heath, *op. cit.*, p. 308. Hipparchus improved the epicyclic theory of Apollonius (pp. 266–267), who had been stimulated by the views of Heraclides of Pontus (p. 274). See also Otto Neugebauer, *Exact Sciences*, p. 155.

144. Lynn Thorndike, *A History of Magic and Experimental Science* (New York: Columbia University Press, 1941), Vol. V, pp. 414–418.

145. Pliny, *Natural History* II 95. See Franz Cumont, *L'Égypte des Astrologues* (Bruselles: Fondation égyptologique Reine Elisabeth, 1937), p. 156. The comment of D. R. Dicks, *The Geographical Fragments of Hipparchus* (London: Athlone Press, 1960), p. 12, on Hipparchus as astrologer is worth quoting: "The idea that one cannot attribute a belief in astrology to a serious student of astronomy without belittling his scientific achievements is as naive as it is unfounded on fact; Kepler cast horoscopes, and it would not be difficult to name prominent modern scientists who, outside their special fields, hold beliefs just as irrational and unscientific as astrology is supposed to be." Backed by Sextus Empiricus, Dicks (p. 14 and Fragment L) states that Hipparchus was probably concerned with "judicial" and geographic astrology and not with the less respectable practice of horoscopic astrology.

146. Martin Nilsson, "The Rise of Astrology in the Hellenistic Age," *Lund-Universitet Observatoriet Meddelanden* (1943) Ser. 2, Vol. XII, No. 111, p. 5.

147. Diogenes Laertius X 134.

CHAPTER THREE: THE ROMAN WORLD

1. Cicero, *de divinatione* II 42–43, cf. I 27–28; *de legibus* II 31, III 27.

2. Cicero, *de senectute* I 11. Cf. Polybius VI 56. Fabius had a Homeric precedent, *Iliad* XII 237–243.

3. Taylor, *op. cit.*, pp. 78–80.

4. Valerius Maximus I 3.3. Livy, *Per.* 54.

5. Strabo II 3.7; 5.26. Cf. VII 3.7.

6. Vitruvius VI 1.9–11.

7. Vergil, *Aeneid* VI 847–853, trans. Rolfe Humphries (New York: Scribner's, 1951), p. 173.

Reference Notes 117

8. Polybius IX 14.4–5. Cf. Sallust, *Jugurthine War* 85.13–14.
8a. Pliny, *Natural History* XVIII 22. Varro, *Res Rusticae* I. 1.10.
9. Cicero, *de republica* I 21–22.
10. Cicero, *Tusculan Disputations* V 64–66. Cf. Plutarch, *Marcellus* 17.
11. Plutarch, *Julius Caesar* 59. Suetonius, *Julius Caesar* 40. Ammianus Marcellinus XXVI 1.13.
12. Suetonius, *Augustus* 31.
13. Pliny, *Natural History* VII 215.
14. Frontinus, *de aquis Romae* I 6. Cf. Strabo V 3.8. Pliny, *Natural History* XXXVI 104–105, 121–123.
15. Pliny, *Natural History* XXVI 100. Celsus, *de medicina* IV 31.
16. Ovid, *Metamorphoses* XV 622–744. Valerius Maximus I 8.2.
17. Pliny, *Natural History* XXIX 12–14. Plutarch, *Cato maior* 23.
18. Cato, *de agri cultura* 160. Charles G. Leland, *Etruscan Roman Remains in Popular Tradition* (New York, 1892), esp. pp. 281–298, showed that Roman remedies and magical practices were still used in nineteenth-century Italy.
19. Pliny, *Natural History* XXVIII 230.
20. Strabo IV 1.5.
21. Cicero, *de officiis* I 151.
22. A. M. Duff, *Freedmen in the Early Roman Empire* (Cambridge: W. Heffer, Ed. 2, 1958), p. 107.
23. Suetonius, *Julius Caesar* 42.
24. Suetonius, *Claudius* 25.
25. Pliny, *Natural History* XXIX 7–8.
26. Tacitus, *Annals* XII 61; 67. Suetonius, *Claudius* 44. Seneca wrote a tasteless satire, *Apocolocyntosis*, on the apotheosis of Claudius.
27. Strabo XII 8.20.
28. Ammianus Marcellinus XXII 16.18.
29. T. R. S. Broughton, "Roman Asia Minor," in *An Economic Survey of Ancient Rome*, ed. Tenney Frank (Baltimore: Johns Hopkins Press, 1938), Vol. IV, p. 851.
30. Suetonius, *Vespasian* 18. Pliny the Younger, *Epistles* X 58.
31. A. C. Johnson, *Ancient Roman Statutes* (Austin: University of Texas Press, 1961), pp. 151, 161. See also William L. Westermann, "The Slave Systems of Greek and Roman Antiquity," *Memoirs of the American Philosophical Society* (1955), Vol. XL, pp. 114–115.
32. Digesta XXVII 1.6.8–12. But see also the petitions of doctors in A. S. Hunt, *Select Papyri* (London: Loeb Classics, 1934), Vol. II, pp. 169, 271.
33. *Scriptores Historiae Augustae*, Severus Alexander 44.4.
34. Pliny, *Natural History* XXXVI 195. Pliny doubts the story which is also found in Petronius, *Satyricon* 51, and Dio Cassius LVII 21.7.
35. See the discussion by R. J. Forbes, *Studies in Ancient Technology* (Leiden: Brill, 1956), Vol. V, pp. 170–172, and F. Lazzenby, "A Note on Vitrum Flexile," *Classical Weekly* (1951) 44:102–103.
36. Tacitus, *Annals* II 87; IV 64; VI 17, 45.
37. Suetonius, *Vespasian* 18.

38. Vitruvius X 5.2. Pliny, *Natural History* XVIII 296. Strabo XII 3.30. *Palatine Anthology* 9.418. See Lynn White Jr., *Medieval Technology and Social Change* (New York: Oxford University Press, 1962), pp. 80–84.
39. See the zealous defense of astrology and other forms of divination by the fourth-century pagan historian, Ammianus Marcellinus XXI 1.8–14.
40. Dio Cassius LVI 25.5.
41. Tacitus, *Histories* I 22, trans. Kenneth Wellesley (London: Penguin Books, 1964), pp. 35–36.
42. Tacitus, *Annals* VI 20–21. Dio Cassius LVII 15.7–8. The careers of Thrasyllus and his son, Balbillus, are well documented by Frederick H. Cramer, "Astrology in Roman Law and Politics," *Memoirs of the American Philosophical Society* (1954), Vol. XXXVII, pp. 92–142.
43. Suetonius, *Tiberius* 62. Dio Cassius LVIII 27.2–3.
44. Suetonius, *Caligula* 19.
45. Suetonius, *Caligula* 12. Philo, *legatio ad Gaium* 6.39–40; 8.59–61.
46. Tacitus, *Annals* VI 22. Suetonius, *Nero* 6. Dio Cassius LXI 2.1–2.
47. Tacitus, *Annals* XIII 22.
48. Suetonius, *Nero* 36.
49. Dio Cassius LXV 9.2.
50. Dio Cassius LXVII 15.6. Suetonius, *Vespasian* 14.
51. Frederick H. Cramer, *op. cit.*, pp. 152–153.
52. Macrobius, *Saturnalia* II 4.21.
53. Suetonius, *Julius Caesar* 56. Cf. Tacitus, *Dialogue on Oratory* 21.
54. Livy IV 20. See Sir Ronald Syme, *The Roman Revolution* (Oxford: Clarendon Press, 1939), pp. 308–309.
55. Sir Ronald Syme, "Livy and Augustus," *Harvard Studies in Classical Philology* (1959) 64:45.
56. Dio Cassius LVI 27.1.
57. Tacitus, *Annals* I 72; IV 34–35. Seutonius, *Caligula* 16.
58. Tacitus, *Agricola* 2.
59. Tacitus, *Agricola* 45. Cf. Pliny the Younger, *Epistles* VIII 14.
60. Pliny, *Natural History* II 117–118.
61. Petronius, *Satyricon* 88.
62. Tacitus, *Dialogue on Oratory* 29, 36–37. Cf. Longinus, *On the Sublime* 44.
63. Aelius Aristides, *Roman Oration* 66.
64. Plutarch, *de pythiae oraculis* 408BCD.
65. C. Kerényi, *Asklepios, Archetypal Image of the Physician's Existence,* trans. Ralph Manheim (New York: Pantheon, 1959), p. 51.
66. Strabo VIII 6.15.
67. Pausanias II 27.1–28.1.
68. Diodorus Siculus I 25.3–5; V 63.2–3; 74.5. Strabo XVII 1.17. See also Arthur D. Knox, *Conversion* (Oxford: Clarendon Press, 1933), pp. 86–88.
69. Lynn Thorndike, *op. cit.*, Vol. I, pp. 139–179. Galen's career and

views are described in T. W. Africa, *Rome of the Caesars* (New York: John Wiley, 1965), pp. 207–220.

70. George Sarton, *Galen of Pergamon* (Lawrence, Kansas: University of Kansas Press, 1954), p. 59, n. 76. Cf. Temkin, *op. cit.*, p. 225.

71. Galen, *On the Natural Faculties* I 12, trans. A. J. Brock (London: Loeb Classics, 1916), pp. 47–49. Cf. I 13, p. 57.

72. T. W. Africa, "The Opium Addiction of Marcus Aurelius," *Journal of the History of Ideas* (1961) 22:97–102. See also E. C. Witke, "Marcus Aurelius and Mandragora," *Classical Philology* (1965) 60:23–24.

72a. William H. Stahl, *Roman Science* (Madison: University of Wisconsin Press, 1962), p. 275 n. 3 and p. 126.

73. Aulus Gellius XIV 1.1–36. Dio Cassius LXIX 11.3. *Scriptores Historiae Augustae*, Hadrian 16.7, Aelius 3.9. See Cramer, *op. cit.*, pp. 168–178.

74. Arnold J. Toynbee, *A Study of History* (London: Oxford University Press and the Royal Institute of International Affairs, 1939), Vol. V, p. 424, n. 1.

75. Frederick H. Cramer, *op. cit.*, p. 247.

76. Aurelius Victor, *de Caesaribus* 41.

77. Otto Neugebauer, *Exact Sciences*, p. 191.

78. *Palatine Anthology* IX 577, trans. Robert Bridges, *The Oxford Book of Greek Verse in Translation*, p. 643.

79. Ptolemy, *Tetrabiblos* I 3.12, trans. F. E. Robbins (London: Loeb Classics, 1940), p. 25.

80. Ptolemy, *Tetrabiblos* II 1.54, trans. Robbins, p. 119.

81. Ptolemy, *Tetrabiblos* II 3.62–63, 65–66, 2.57.

82. Sir James Frazer, *The New Golden Bough*, ed. T. H. Gaster (New York: Criterion Books, 1959), p. 648. Copyright (c) 1959 by S. G. Phillips, Inc.

83. Lynn Thorndike, "The True Place of Astrology in the History of Science," *Isis* (1955) 46:273–278.

84. Charles N. Cochrane, *Christianity and Classical Culture* (New York: Oxford University Press, 1957), p. 2.

85. *Scriptores Historiae Augustae*, Septimius Severus 3.9, Geta 2.6–7, Severus Alexander 27.5. Dio Cassius LXXVII 11.1. Herodian IV 12.3.

86. Porphyry, *Life of Plotinus* 10; 15. See Philip Merlan, "Plotinus and Magic," *Isis* (1953) 44:341–348, and E. R. Dodds, *op. cit.*, pp. 283–311.

87. Porphyry, *Life of Plotinus* 12.

88. Robert M. Grant, *Miracle and Natural Law in Graeco-Roman and Early Christian Thought* (Amsterdam: North Holland Publishing Company, 1952), p. 116.

89. Eusebius, *Ecclesiastical History* VII 32.6–21. See J. Heiberg, *Anatolius sur les dix premiers nombres* (Macon: Protat Frères, 1901).

90. Eusebius, *Ecclesiastical History* V 28.14–15.

91. Suidas, "Chemistry," trans. Arthur J. Hopkins, *Alchemy: Child of Greek Philosophy* (New York: Columbia University Press, 1934) p.

246. Lynn Thorndike, *History of Magic*, Vol. I, p. 194, doubts the story.

92. Firmicus Maternus, *Mathesis* II 30.4, trans. Cramer, *op. cit.* p. 279.

93. Theodosian Code IX 16.8. Cf. 16.12.

94. Ammianus Marcellinus XXIII 4.1–15; 6.37–38.

95. Tacitus, *Annals* XII 45.

96. Zosimus V 21.2.

97. Procopius, *Gothic Wars* VIII 11.27–31.

98. Lynn White Jr., "Technology and Invention in the Middle Ages," *Speculum* (1940) 15:144.

99. *De rebus bellicis*, preface 4, II 2–3., trans. E. A. Thompson, *A Roman Reformer and Inventor* (Oxford: Clarendon Press, 1952) pp. 106–107, 110.

100. *De rebus bellicis* XVII 1–3 and Figure XI.

101. Ammianus Marcellinus XXX 9.4. Aurelius Victor, *de Caesaribus* 45.

102. Marshall Clagett, *Greek Science in Antiquity* (New York: Collier, 1963), p. 45.

103. Ammianus Marcellinus XXII 16.17, trans. John Rolfe (London: Loeb Classics, 1956), Vol. II, pp. 305–307. Cf. the book burnings in the Eastern provinces under the emperor Valens—Ammianus Marcellinus XXIX 2.4.

103a. Ammianus Marcellinus XXII 16.15 mentions great destruction in the vicinity of the Library during the reign of Aurelian, but it need not be inferred that the Library itself suffered any great loss. In its long history, Alexandria was often the scene of disorders, but the Library seems to have survived them all, and reports of its repeated "destruction" were obviously exaggerated.

104. Orosius VI 15.31.

105. Edward A. Parsons, *op. cit.*, pp. 371–421, exhaustively discusses this controversial event.

106. Tertullian, *de praescriptione* 7; *de testimonio animae* 1; 5, trans. Charles N. Cochrane, *op. cit.*, pp. 222–223.

107. *Didascalia apostolorum* XII, trans. M. L. Laistner, *Christianity and Pagan Culture in the Later Roman Empire* (Ithaca: Cornell University Press, 1951), p. 50. Copyright (c) 1951 by Cornell University. Used by permission of Cornell University Press.

108. Arnobius, *adversus gentes* II 61, trans. Grant, *op. cit.*, p. 113.

109. Hans Lietzmann, *A History of the Early Church* (New York: Meridian, 1961), Vol. III, pp. 255–256.

110. Augustine, *Confessions* V 4.

111. Cf. Psalm 148.4.

112. Cf. Proverbs 8.27–28.

113. Romans 10.18. Cf. Psalm 19.4.

114. Lactantius, *Divine Institutes* III 24. The antipodes were also rejected by two reputable pagans, Lucretius I 1052–1067 and Plutarch, *de facie quae in orbe lunae apparet* 924A, but cf. *de Herodoti malignitate* 869C.

115. Lynn Thorndike, *History of Magic*, Vol. I, p. 481.
116. J. L. E. Dreyer, *op. cit.*, p. 210.
117. Ambrose, *Hexameron* II 3.9; VI 2.8.
118. Augustine, *Confessions* XIII 32. Cf. *City of God* XI 34.
119. Augustine, *Retractiones* II 6.2.
120. Augustine, *de Genesi ad litteram* II 5.
121. John K. Wright, *The Geographical Lore of the Time of the Crusades* (New York: American Geographical Society, 1925), pp. 53–57, 383–386.
122. J. B. Bury, *Later Roman Empire*, Vol. I, pp. 217–219, blames Bishop Cyril for the murder of Hypatia. J. M. Rist, "Hypatia," *Phoenix* (1965) 19:214–225, exonerates Cyril despite the consensus of ancient writers on Hypatia.
123. M. A. Huttmann, "The Establishment of Christianity and the Proscription of Paganism," *Columbia University Studies in History* (1914), Vol. CXLVII, pp. 248–249.
124. J. B. Bury, *Later Roman Empire*, Vol. II, pp. 369–370. See also A. H. M. Jones, *The Later Roman Empire* (Norman: University of Oklahoma Press, 1964), Vol. II, pp. 938–941, on education and Christian suppression of paganism.
125. T. E. Mommsen, "Petrarch's Conception of the 'Dark Ages,'" *Speculum* (1942) 17:226–242.
126. *Excerpta Valesiana* 14.79. For the background of this tragedy, see William Bark, "Theodoric vs. Boethius: Vindication and Apology," *American Historical Review* (1944) 49:410–426, and "The Legend of Boethius' Martyrdom," *Speculum* (1946) 21:312–317.
127. *Excerpta Valesiana* 14.87. Although he executed the philosopher Boethius and the historian Symmachus, Theodoric was an able ruler and a patron of culture. See William H. Stahl, *op. cit.*, pp. 193–198, J. B. Bury, *op. cit.*, Vol. I, p. 467, and the cautionary observation of A. H. M. Jones, *op. cit.*, Vol. I, pp. 264–265.
128. Procopius, *Anecdota* VI 15–16.
129. Benjamin Farrington, *Science and Politics*, p. 21.
130. Aristotle, *Metaphysics* I 2.982b.
131. Thomas Aquinas, *Summa Theologica*, I Q. 68, Art. 3; Q. 70, Art. 1, but see also Q. 102, Art. 1, on the historicity of Eden.
132. William H. Stahl, *Roman Science* (Madison: University of Wisconsin Press, 1962), is a useful study of the Latin handbook tradition and its influence in the Dark Ages.
133. F. A. Wright, ed. and trans., *The Works of Liudprand of Cremona* (London: G. Routledge, 1930), pp. 235, 254.
134. *Ibid.*, pp. 207–208.
135. M. I. Finley, "Technological Innovation and Economic Progress in the Ancient World," *Economic History Review* (1965) 18:29–45.
136. A. G. Drachmann, *Mechanical Technology*, p. 206.
137. Michael Rostovtzeff, *The Social and Economic History of the Roman Empire* (Oxford: Clarendon Press, Ed. 2, 1957), Vol. I, pp. 350–351.

138. Kenneth R. Stampp, *The Peculiar Institution* (New York: Knopf, 1956), pp. 64–67.
139. *Ibid.*, pp. 426–428. Marcus M. Tod, *The Cambridge Ancient History*, Vol. V, p. 25. M. I. Finley, *Historia* (1959) 8:155.
140. Derek J. de Solla Price, *op. cit.*, pp. 38–42, and "An Ancient Greek Computer," *Scientific American* (June 1959) 200:60–67. Cf. Lynn White Jr., *Medieval Technology*, pp. 79–82.
141. Plutarch, *Alexander* 35. Michael Rostovtzeff, *Hellenistic World*, Vol. II, p. 1176; Vol. III, p. 1614, n. 126. See also Vitruvius VIII 3.8, and Diodorus Siculus XIX 98–99 (based on Hieronymus of Cardia).
142. Pliny, *Natural History* XXXIV 10–11. See F. Oertel, *The Cambridge Ancient History*, Vol. X, pp. 391–392.
143. Michael Rostovtzeff, *Roman Empire*, Vol. I, p. 352.
144. Michael Rostovtzeff, *Hellenistic World*, Vol. II, p. 1237.

APPENDIX: A HISTORIOGRAPHICAL NOTE

 1. Strabo XV 1.2. Cf. 1.68.
 2. Diodorus Siculus I 39.7; 41.4–9.
 3. Plutarch, *Demosthenes* 2, *Alexander* 1, *Cimon* 2, *Solon* 27.
 4. Plutarch, *Pericles* 32.
 5. Plutarch, *Cimon* 13. Cf. Philochorus (Jacoby 328 F 151).
 6. Athenaeus XIV 657F. Cf. XII 549D.
 7. Plato, *Gorgias* 470D, 472A, 473F, 503C.
 8. See the excellent discussion by James Day and Mortimer Chambers, *Aristotle's History of Athenian Democracy* (Berkeley: University of California Press, 1962).
 9. Thucydides I 1. For a defense of the historian, see A. W. Gomme, *A Historical Commentary on Thucydides* (Oxford: Clarendon Press, 1945), Vol. I, pp. 89–90.
10. Herodotus III 80. Cf. VI 43. See also VII 152; II 123.

PERMISSIONS

The author wishes to thank the following individuals and publishers for their permission to reprint copyright material:

American Elsevier Publishing Company:
  Edward A. Parsons, *The Alexandrian Library*, 1952.
American Philosophical Society:
  Frederick H. Cramer, *Astrology in Roman Law and Politics*, 1954.
Bobbs-Merrill Company:
  Plato's Epistles, translated by Glenn R. Morrow, 1962.
Brown University Press:
  Otto Neugebauer, *The Exact Sciences in Antiquity*, 1957.
Cambridge University Press:
  Joseph Needham, *Science and Civilization in China*, 1959.
Clarendon Press:
  Aristotle, *Politics*, translated by Ernest Barker, 1952.
  Aristotle, *Parts of Animals*, translated by William Ogle, 1912.
  Charles N. Cochrane, *Christianity and Classical Culture*, 1944.
  Oxford Book of Greek Verse in Translation, 1953.
  Michael Rostovtzeff, *Social and Economic History of the Hellenistic World*, 1952.
  E. A. Thompson, *A Roman Reformer and Inventor*, 1952.
Columbia University Press:
  Arthur J. Hopkins, *Alchemy: Child of Greek Philosophy*, 1934.
Cornell University Press:
  M. L. Laistner, *Christianity and Pagan Culture in the Later Roman Empire*, 1951.
Harvard University Press:
  I. E. Drabkin and Morris Cohen, *A Source Book in Greek Science*, 1958.
  Ammianus Marcellinus, translated by John Rolfe, Loeb Classics, 1956.
  Galen, *On Natural Faculties*, translated by A. J. Brock, Loeb Classics, 1916.
  Diogenes Laertius, translated by R. D. Hicks, Loeb Classics, 1931.
Methuen and Company and Harper and Row:
  Adolf Erman, *The Literature of the Ancient Egyptians*, translated by Aylward M. Blackman, 1927.
Oxford University Press and the Royal Institute of International Affairs:
  Arnold J. Toynbee, *A Study of History*, 1939.

Penguin Books, Ltd.:
  Plutarch, *Rise and Fall of Athens*, translated by Ian Scott-Kilvert, 1960.
  Liu Wu-Chi, *A Short History of Confucian Philosophy*, 1955.
S. G. Phillips, Inc.:
  James G. Frazer, *The New Golden Bough*, edited by T. H. Gaster, 1959.
Routledge and Kegan Paul, Ltd.:
  F. A. Wright, *The Works of Liudprand of Cremona*, 1930.
University of California Press:
  Frank Adcock, *The Greek and Macedonian Art of War*, 1957.
The University of Chicago Press:
  Wolfram Eberhard in *Chinese Thought and Institutions*, 1957.
  Edgar J. Goodspeed, *The Apocrypha*, 1938.
University of Oklahoma Press:
  J. Eric Thompson, *The Rise and Fall of Maya Civilization*, 1954.
Mrs. R. H. Webb and the University Press of Virginia:
  Aristophanes, *The Birds*, translated by R. H. Webb, 1962.
Yale University Press:
  Karl Wittfogel, *Oriental Despotism*, 1957.

Index

Hecataeus, 22
Hegesias, 55
Heraclitus, 21, 25
Hercules, 17
Hermias, 24
Hero, 51, 63, 94
Herodotus, 9, 21, 22, 26, 99
Herophilus, 50, 51
Hesiod, 18, 34
Hiero II, 49, 52
Hillyer, R., 86
Hipparchus, 66, 79, 92, 116
Hippias, 27
Hippocrates, 23
"Hippocratic" Oath, 23
Hippodamus, 41
Homer, 10, 16, 17, 26, 34
Hypatia, 89, 121

Icarus, 18, 91, 92
Imhotep, 10
India, 6
Isocrates, 27
Itzcoatl, 8

Jaeger, W., 25
Justin, 90
Justinian, 89, 90

Kepler, J., 37, 65
Kerenyi, C., 77

Lactantius, 88
Leonardo da Vinci, 61
Library, Alexandrian, 54, 55, 86,
112, 120
Liudprand, 93
Livy, 76, 113
Lucretius, 120

Machaon, 16, 24
Macro, 74, 75
Magi, Three, 54, 112
Mago, 70
Mandocles, 22
Marcus Aurelius, 78
Marx, K., 9

Mayans, 6, 7
Megalophanes, 34
Megasthenes, 6
Melissus, 42
Meno, 98
Meredith, G., 67
Mesopotamia, 11–13
Meton, 39–41
Milo, 23, 31
Milton, J., 82, 96
Mochus, 8
Museum, Alexandrian, 50, 55–56, 64,
85, 86, 92, 96
Mycenaeans, 16

Necho, 53
Neleus, 55
Nero, 75
Neugenauer, O., 3
Newton, I., 81
Nicias, 39
Nicolaus of Damascus, 54
Nicomachus, 24
Nilsson, M., 66

Old Testament, 87, 88
Onesicritus, 62
Orosius, 86

Panaetius, 48, 65, 98
Paul, Saint, 64, 87
Pausanias, 77
Pergamum, 54
Pericles, 39, 42, 43, 57
Periläus, 18, 19
Petrarch, 89
Petronius, 76
Phalaris, 18, 19, 103
Philip of Macedon, 25, 27, 28, 57
Philo, 60
Philolaus, 32
Philopappus, 75
Philostratus, 57
Phormio, 60
Plague, Athenian, 41, 109
Plato, 14, 21, 24, 27, 32–35, 37, 38,
42, 43, 65, 89, 98, 108